Canada, Aboriginal Peoples,
and Residential Schools

They Came
for the Children

"

In order to educate the children properly
we must separate them from their families.
Some people may say that this is hard but if
we want to civilize them we must do that.

"

Hector Langevin,
Public Works Minister of Canada, 1883

Truth and
Reconciliation
Commission of Canada

2012

Truth and Reconciliation Commission of Canada
1500-360 Main Street
Winnipeg, Manitoba
R3C 3Z3

Telephone: (204) 984-5885
Toll Free: 1-888-872-5554 (1-888-TRC-5554)
Fax: (204) 984-5915

Email: info@trc.ca
Website: www.trc.ca

Library and Archives Canada Cataloguing in Publication

      They came for the children : Canada, Aboriginal peoples, and residential schools.

Issued also in French under title: Ils sont venus pour les enfants.
Includes bibliographical references.
Available also on the Internet.
ISBN 978-1-100-19995-5
Cat. no.: IR4-4/2012E

      1. Native peoples--Canada--Residential schools. 2. Native peoples--Canada--History. 3. Native peoples--Abuse of--Canada. 4. Native children--Abuse of--Canada. 5. Native peoples--Crimes against--Canada. 6. Native children--Crimes against--Canada. 7. Native peoples--Cultural assimilation--Canada. 8. Native peoples--Canada--Government relations. I. Truth and Reconciliation Commission of Canada II. Title: Canada, Aboriginal peoples, and residential schools.

E96.5 T43 2012   371.829'97071   C2012-980022-8

Cover photographs: Clockwise starting from the upper left: Department of Indian Affairs and Northern Development fonds, Library and Archives Canada, 1973-357, Shingle Point, 1930; a102086; The General Synod Archives, Anglican Church of Canada, M2008-10 (P14), Gordon's school, 1953; P75-103 (S7-184), Old Sun School, 1945; P2004-09 (348), St. Cyprian's School, 1952.

Design: Doowah Design Inc.

 Truth and Reconciliation Commission of Canada | Commission de vérité et réconciliation du Canada

trc.ca

December 31, 2011
The Parties of the Indian Residential Schools Settlement Agreement

To the Parties,

The Truth and Reconciliation Commission of Canada is pleased to submit this Report on the history, purpose, operation, and supervision of the residential school system, the effect and consequences of the system, and its ongoing legacy, as required by the Commission's mandate.

This Report was prepared in compliance with the Commission's obligation to prepare such a Report at the two-year point of its mandate. However, it has had to have been written without a review of government and church documents, as the Commission has experienced significant delays in the collection and receipt of those documents. In addition, the gathering of statements from survivors and those otherwise involved in the schools is ongoing. The Commission anticipates that once an analysis of those documents and statements has been compiled, more historical information will become available. Based on that and its ongoing research, the Commission will be submitting a fuller and more detailed report, along with a complete set of recommendations, at the completion of its full five-year mandate.

Yours respectfully,

Justice Murray Sinclair
Chair of the Truth and Reconciliation Commission of Canada

Chief Wilton Littlechild
Commissioner

Marie Wilson
Commissioner

1500-360 Main Street
Winnipeg, Manitoba R3C 3Z3
Tel: 204.984.5885
Fax: 204.984.5915

Contents

Preface

The Truth and Reconciliation Commission of Canada is publishing this history as a part of its mandate to educate the Canadian public about residential schools and their place in Canadian history.

The Commission was established by the Indian Residential Schools Settlement Agreement. The agreement was reached in response to numerous class-action lawsuits that former students of residential schools had brought against the federal government and the churches that operated those schools in Canada for well over 100 years. The Truth and Reconciliation Commission has been mandated to inform all Canadians about what happened in the schools and to guide a process of national reconciliation.

For the child taken, and for the parent left behind, we encourage Canadians to read this history, to understand the legacy of the schools, and to participate in the work of reconciliation.

Introduction

This book tells a painful story.

For over a century, generations of Aboriginal children were separated from their parents and raised in over-crowded, underfunded, and often unhealthy residential schools across Canada. They were commonly denied the right to speak their language and told their cultural beliefs were sinful. Some students did not see their parents for years. Others—the victims of scandalously high death rates—never made it back home. Even by the standards of the day, discipline often was excessive. Lack of supervision left students prey to sexual predators. To put it simply: the needs of tens of thousands of Aboriginal children were neglected routinely. Far too many children were abused far too often.

But this story is about more than neglect and abuse. Those painful stories rightfully have captured national headlines. They are central to the story this book tells. But there is more to tell.

This is a story of loss.

Residential schools disrupted families and communities. They prevented elders from teaching children long-valued cultural and spiritual traditions and practices. They helped kill languages. These were not side effects of a well-intentioned system: the purpose of the residential school system was to separate children from the influences of their parents and their community, so as to destroy their culture. The impact was devastating. Countless students emerged from the schools as lost souls, their lives soon to be cut short by drugs, alcohol, and violence. The last of the federally supported schools and residences, of which there were at least 150, closed in the 1990s.*

For Canada, this is a shameful story.

The Canadian government took on heavy responsibilities when it established residential schools. Education, it was said, would "civilize" Aboriginal people. Children were to be fed and housed, and taught skills and trades that would allow them to support themselves and their families. But once the schools had been established, politicians discovered they had underestimated the cost of running a humane and effective system. They knew from the earliest days that the schools were failing to provide children with the education they needed and the care they deserved. Despite this, government after government lacked either the courage to fund the schools properly or

---

* The 2007 Indian Residential Schools Settlement Agreement identified 134 residential school and residences. Former students who attended these institutions on a residential basis were eligible to make compensation claims under the settlement agreement. Since the agreement was reached, former students have applied to have over 1300 schools added to the list. Eight of these applications have been accepted to date (August 31, 2011). The vast majority of applications have been rejected. In August 2011, the Ontario Supreme Court of Justice ordered that two more schools be added to the list. At least nine other schools were not included in the settlement agreement because they closed in the early twentieth century. In addition, many students attended residential schools, but did not live at them. Day students have initiated court action seeking compensation for their school experiences. Students who attended boarding schools in Labrador have launched similar court actions. The stories of both these groups are yet to be told.

the initiative to close them down. Drift and inertia took the place of vision.

It is also a story about the response to a sacred call.

For most of the system's history, the residential schools were operated by religious organizations. Priests, nuns, ministers, and missionaries organized the schools, taught the classes, and took care of the students from morning to night. Almost always, they were overworked and underpaid. They took on this difficult life because they felt they were answering a sacred call to spread the Christian faith around the world. They dedicated their lives to this missionary work.

It is a story about Canadian colonialism.

While many people who worked in the schools were inspired by an impulse to "save" and to "civilize" Canada's Aboriginal people, government had other motives. To gain control of Aboriginal land, the Canadian government signed treaties it did not respect, took over land without making treaties, and unilaterally passed laws that controlled nearly every aspect of Aboriginal life. No other Canadians were subject to this level of regulation. No word better describes these policies than "colonialism." The schools were central to the colonization of the Aboriginal peoples of Canada.

It is a complicated story.

It would be wrong and foolish to say that no Aboriginal people benefited from the schools. Many have come forward to the Truth and Reconciliation Commission to express their gratitude to the men and women who worked in the schools. Although the overall educational outcomes of the schools were limited, the system was not without its accomplishments. Human connections were made. Doors were opened, and opportunities created. People applied themselves, overcame tremendous barriers, and developed skills they were able to draw upon for the rest of their lives.

It is a story of humility and the possibility of change.

Beginning in 1986, Canadian churches began to apologize for attempting to impose European culture and values on Aboriginal people. Apologies specific to the operation of residential schools came soon after. On June 11, 2008, Prime Minister Stephen Harper issued an apology to former residential school students on behalf of all Canadians. His statement recognized that the primary purpose of the schools had been to remove children from their homes and families in order to assimilate them into the dominant culture. Such a policy, he said, was wrong, and had no place in this country.

Most importantly, this story is a tribute to Aboriginal resilience: a determination not just to endure, but to flourish.

The residential schools were intended to bring about the end of Aboriginal people as a distinct group within Canadian society. That effort failed. Aboriginal parents and children continuously resisted residential schooling. Aboriginal people wanted educational opportunities. They insisted that schools be included in treaties. But they wanted them in their own communities, and expected they would be respectful of Aboriginal culture. In the 1980s, former students, who referred to themselves as "survivors" of residential schools, began to draw the residential school history to public attention. They had few resources available to help them in this work. Some established support groups, some launched lawsuits, and many came forward to speak of their school experiences at the hearings held by the Canadian Royal Commission on Aboriginal Peoples. Their efforts culminated in 2007 with the court approval of the Indian Residential Schools Settlement Agreement, the largest class-action settlement in Canadian history. Along with providing compensation for former residential school students, the agreement required the establishment of the Indian Residential Schools Truth and Reconciliation Commission. Through their courage and determination, the survivors are succeeding in bringing this story to light.

It is a story about how, in crucial ways, our schools failed all of us.

For much of our history, all Canadian children—Aboriginal and non-Aboriginal alike—were taught that Aboriginal people were inferior, savage, and uncivilized, and that Aboriginal languages, spiritual beliefs, and ways of life were irrelevant. Aboriginal people were depicted as having been a dying race, saved from destruction by the intervention of humanitarian Europeans. Since little that was taught about Aboriginal people was positive, the system led non-Aboriginal people to believe they were inherently superior.

This is a story of destruction carried out in the name of civilization.

Residential schools were justified by arguments that they would assist Aboriginal people in making the leap to civilization. It is still argued by some that while residential schools may have been unpleasant, at least they helped Aboriginal people become civilized. This, it was said, was the price of progress. These views are not acceptable. They are based on a belief that societies can be ranked in value. In this ranking system, Aboriginal societies are described as primitive and savage. European societies judged themselves as having progressed to the top of the scale, and pronounced themselves civilized. This determination of whether a society could be termed "civilized" supposedly was made on the basis of such criteria as level of social organization, moral and ethical advancement, and technological achievement. In reality, it was a highly biased judgment, usually made by a powerful society about a less powerful one whose lands and resources it coveted and whose social and cultural differences it either misunderstood or feared.

The destruction and transformation of Aboriginal societies, which was unleashed in the name of civilization, did not constitute progress for the people who lived in those societies. They already had an effective understanding of their environment. They had developed practices and technologies to draw a long-term livelihood from it efficiently. They each had a set of spiritual beliefs that provided coherence to their lives. They had social structures based on well-developed principles and values. Their societies were not without violence and social problems, but neither were the societies that sought to civilize them. The process of "civilizing" was, in reality, the process of destroying a continent full of civilizations.

This is our story and Canada's story.

In talking about residential schools and their legacy, we are not talking about an Aboriginal problem, but a Canadian problem. It is not simply a dark chapter from our past. It was integral to the making of Canada. Although the schools are no longer in operation, the last ones did not close until the 1990s. The colonial framework

of which they were a central element has not been dismantled. One can see its impact in the social, economic, and political challenges that Aboriginal communities struggle with every day. It is present also in the attitudes that too often shape the relations between Aboriginal and non-Aboriginal peoples in Canada.

This story is not over.

The history recounted in this book will cause many Canadians to see their country differently. It is painful to discover that, as a nation, we have not always lived up to our ideals or the image we seek to project on the international stage. That does not mean we should abandon our ideals. We cannot change the past, but the future is in our hands. We are called to undertake the ongoing work of reconciliation: to right the relationship between Aboriginal and non-Aboriginal Canada. This is no easy or straightforward task. We need to revive old visions in which these communities came together in a spirit of sharing and mutual exchange. The Truth and Reconciliation Commission will be seeking to guide this process throughout the rest of its mandate. We encourage Canadians to read this history, participate in Commission events, and, in the coming years, to join in the ongoing task of coming to grips with our nation's past and charting a future in which we can all take pride.

Justice Murray Sinclair
Chair, Truth and Reconciliation Commission of Canada

Chief Wilton Littlechild
Commissioner, Truth and Reconciliation Commission of Canada

Marie Wilson
Commissioner, Truth and Reconciliation Commission of Canada

CHAPTER ONE

To Christianize and Civilize: Canada's Residential Schools

Students played a major role in building the facilities at the Battleford school (photographed here in 1895). In 1889 the principal reported that students had built the bakery and the carpenter's shop, converted the attic to dormitories, and put up a fence separating the boys' and girls' playground. *David Ewens Collection, Library and Archives Canada, PA-182266.*

In 1883, Sir John A. Macdonald, who was both Canada's prime minister and minister of Indian Affairs, moved a measure through his cabinet authorizing the creation of three residential schools for Aboriginal children in the Canadian West. The plan was for two Roman Catholic schools, one at Qu'Appelle (in what is now Saskatchewan) and one at High River (in what is now southwestern Alberta), and an Anglican school in Battleford (in what is now Saskatchewan).[1] In announcing the plan, Public Works Minister Hector Langevin told the House of Commons, "In order to educate the children properly we must separate them from their families. Some people may say that this is hard but if we want to civilize them we must do that."[2]

These three were not the first residential schools for Aboriginal people in Canada. Missionaries from France began laying the groundwork for the residential school system as early as 1620, but it did not take root. Parents were reluctant to send their children to the boarding schools that Roman Catholic missionaries had opened. The few children they did recruit ran away to rejoin their families as soon as they could. The French boarding school experiment was abandoned long before the British conquest of 1763.[3]

The idea was not revived fully until the 1830s, when the Mohawk Institute in Brantford, Ontario, founded by the New England Company, a British-based missionary society, began boarding First Nations students. In 1850 Methodist missionaries opened the Mount Elgin school in Munceytown, Ontario. From its establishment in 1867, the Canadian government funded these two schools. In the 1870s, Jesuit missionaries opened boarding schools for boys and girls at Wikwemikong on Manitoulin Island, while Anglicans did the same at Sault Ste. Marie. In addition to these schools in eastern Canada, Catholic and Protestant missionaries established schools on the Pacific coast, the Prairies, and in the North.

What existed prior to 1883 was not a residential school system, but a series of individual church-led initiatives to which the federal government provided grants. The federal government decision in that year to open three new schools on the Prairies marked a break from this practice and the beginning of Canada's residential school system. Although federal officials let the churches run the Qu'Appelle, High River, and Battleford schools, the government built them, appointed the principals (on church recommendations), and paid most of their operating costs.[4] These three new schools were called "industrial schools." They were expected to prepare older students for assimilation into Euro-Canadian society by training them in a range of trades including printing and boot-making, and the garment trade, along with a basic education in farming, carpentry, cooking, and housework.

The industrial schools were deliberately located away from reserves, and were intended to complement the smaller church-run boarding schools. Those boarding schools provided a more basic education, and usually were located on reserves, but at a distance from Aboriginal settlements.[5] Neither industrial schools nor boarding schools offered high-school education. In addition to these schools, the federal government and the churches also operated day schools on reserves across Canada. There were always more day schools than residential schools and usually more day-school students than residential-school students.

Funding was a problem from the outset. When Macdonald gave Indian Affairs the $44,000 needed to build the first three schools, he actually cut the department's budget by $140,000 in that year. As a result of these cuts, Indian Affairs reduced the already meagre relief rations it was providing to western Aboriginal people at a time when they were facing starvation following the disappearance of the buffalo.[6]

Over the next fifty years, the residential school system grew dramatically. By 1931 the government was funding eighty schools. This increase in the number of schools was a central part of Canada's western and northern expansion, and of the colonization of the Aboriginal population of Canada's new lands.

Prime Minister John A. Macdonald, 1868. Macdonald believed it was necessary to separate Aboriginal children from their parents in residential schools. In 1883 he told the House of Commons, "When the school is on the reserve, the child lives with his parents who are savages; he is surrounded by savages, and though he may learn to read and write, his habits and training and mode of thought are Indian. He is simply a savage who can read and write." *Library and Archives Canada, Harold Daly fonds, C-006513.*

Residential Schools and the Taming of the West

Canada's westward and northern expansion began in 1870 when Rupert's Land was transferred from the Hudson's Bay Company to Canada. In today's terms, this area of land included much of northern Quebec and Ontario, all of Manitoba, most of Saskatchewan, southern Alberta, and a portion of the Northwest Territories and Nunavut. For the Canadian government, the prairie West was the jewel in this imperial crown. Settling the plains would create a large domestic market for eastern Canadian industry, raise grain for export, and provide a route for a railway to the Pacific.[7] It was on the basis of the promise of the rail line that British Columbia joined Confederation in 1871, linking the country from sea to sea.

The Canadian government distributed these medals at the signing of treaties with the Aboriginal people of the plains. The sun rising on the horizon indicated that the treaties were meant to last forever.

Library and Archives Canada, Department of Indian Affairs and Northern Development fonds, e000009998.

Aboriginal people made up the vast majority of the residents of the new North-West Territories. Before Aboriginal lands could be transferred to settlers, there was a legal requirement that the Crown first deal with the Aboriginal title to the land. This was accomplished by the negotiation of a treaty with the First Nations. Prior to Confederation in 1867, the British government had negotiated numerous treaties with Aboriginal nations in eastern Canada. While the first of these treaties were concluded on the basis of one-time-only payments, later treaties included reserves (an area of often remote land set aside for specific bands of Aboriginal people) and annual payments.

The need for prairie treaties was pressing, since Aboriginal people were resistant to the growing Canadian presence. For example, the Ojibway in what is now northwestern Ontario opposed the ongoing passage of settlers through their territory, the Plains Ojibway turned back settlers at Portage la Prairie, and the Plains Cree halted the construction of telegraph lines.[8] In 1870, when the United States was spending $20-million on its Indian wars, Canada's total national budget was $19-million. Since Canada could not afford an Indian war, treaty commissioners were sent out, accompanied by soldiers and, later, police officers.[9]

Between 1871 and 1877, Aboriginal people from northwestern Ontario through to southwestern Alberta signed seven treaties. Aboriginal negotiators were seeking economic security in a period of dramatic change and crisis. Eventually, they won provisions for medical care, livestock, schools, teachers, farm instructors, transportation, clothing, and, when needed, relief. The government negotiators also left the people with the impression they would be allowed to continue to live off the resources of their lands. By 1884 Cree leaders meeting at Duck Lake in what is now Saskatchewan concluded that the treaties were deceptions, nothing more than "sweet promises" intended to lull them into giving up their land. Reality had proven to be far more bitter. The Plains Cree found themselves forced onto small, isolated reserves. Restrictions were placed on their movement. The promised farm equipment arrived only after long delay, and often was of poor quality. The farm instructors often were incompetent. The rations, when provided, were inadequate.[10] The Numbered Treaties and the Pre-Confederation Treaties, reached between the Crown and sovereign First Nations, were the equivalent of international treaties. Treating them as anything less reflects a colonialist attitude and ignores the viewpoint of the Aboriginal negotiators. First Nation leaders entered into the Treaty making process for the purpose of establishing a relationship of respect that included an ongoing set of mutual obligations including land sharing based on kinship and cooperation. For its part, the Canadian government saw the treaties only as land transfer agreements. The government's policy was one of assimilation under which it sought to remove any First Nations legal interest in the land, while reducing and ignoring its own treaty obligations. Schooling was expected to play a central role in achieving that policy goal.

Aboriginal Peoples and Education

Historically Aboriginal people throughout North America lived in successful and dynamic societies. These societies had their own languages, history, cultures, spirituality, technologies, and values. The security and survival of these societies depended on passing on this cultural legacy from one generation to the next. Aboriginal peoples did this successfully through a seamless mixture of teachings, ceremonies, and daily activities.[11] While differing in specifics from one people to another, traditional Aboriginal teachings described a coherent, interconnected world. Not only did they account for the creation of human beings, animals, and the physical world, they described the role that supernatural beings—often shape-changing tricksters with the power to do good or harm—played in shaping the relationship among humans, animals, and the landscape.[12] There was no rigid separation of daily secular life and spiritual life. For example, in some cultures, animals were said to give themselves as gifts to the hunter. To be worthy of receiving the gift, the hunter had to participate in a ceremony prior to and after the hunt.[13]

Ceremonial feasts could bring people together for a variety of spiritual, cultural, and economic purposes. At such feasts, people could fulfill spiritual commitments, exchange goods and information, and impart traditional teachings.[14] Elders were the keepers and transmitters of this knowledge, and in some cases medicine people had specific roles in dealing with the spirit world and in curing the sick.[15] Just as spiritual life was part of daily activity rather than confined to a church, education was woven into everyday activities. In this way, living and learning were integrated. Children learned through storytelling, through example, and by participation in rituals, festivals, and individual coming-of-age ceremonies. In some cultures, there were spiritual societies with specific positions to which people could be promoted after undergoing proper instruction.[16] This teaching method was strong enough to assure the survival of identity, history, traditions, and beliefs.

Through story, children were taught how to live correctly, how not to offend spirits, and how to contribute to the community's physical survival. Angela Sidney, a Tlingit woman from the Yukon Territory in the early twentieth century, said, "They used to teach us with stories. They teach us what is good, what is bad, things like that.... Those days they told stories mouth to mouth. That's how they educate people."[17] Albert Canadien, who grew up fifty years later in a Dene community on the Mackenzie River, received the same sort of education: "I heard many stories that provided some explanation for why we must do certain things and why things were the way they were. A story was much better than an adult simply saying, 'You do this because I told you so!' Children tend to listen and be a little more attentive to stories than to rules."[18] Growing up in a Mi'kmaw community in Nova Scotia in the 1930s, Isabelle Knockwood was taught to revere elders and their knowledge: "They knew the seasonal cycles of edible and medicinal plants, and the migrations of animals, birds and fish, and they knew which hunting and trapping methods worked best with certain weather conditions."[19]

Hamasaka in Tlu Wulahu costume with Speaker's Staff - Qagyuhl, British Columbia, approximately 1914. Elders played a key role in the education of Aboriginal children. *Library and Archives Canada, Edward S. Curtis, Edward Curtis's The North American Indian collection, C-020826.*

From an early age, children contributed to the survival of the community. In the early twentieth century, Mary John, a Carrier woman from the British Columbia interior, took care of younger brothers and sisters while she was still a youngster, and her older sister learned to dry and smoke fish, and to hunt.[20] The young Inuit girl Masak was taught by her grandmother how to scrape skins, and cut and sew mukluks.[21] Born in 1942 in western Manitoba, Raphael Ironstand spent much of his early life travelling with his mother and father in the Duck Mountain region, living off the land. On the night before a hunt, his father would bring out the hand drum and sing traditional songs in a slow, soft voice. According to Ironstand, his father "was a survivor, using all his cunning and native guile as he tracked and stalked game for food, singing his songs when he was closing in on the prey."[22]

Coming-of-age ceremonies could include vision quests, in which young men, after undergoing a period of

Ojibway woman with child in carrier basket, 1858. Missionaries across North America commented on the close bond between Aboriginal parents and their children. A seventeenth-century missionary, Gabriel Sagard, observed, "They love their children dearly." *Library and Archives Canada, Humphrey Lloyd Hime, National Archives of Canada fonds, C-000728.*

privation, might acquire a guardian spirit or experience a vision that promised them invincibility in war or long life.[23]

Because personal autonomy was highly regarded, scolding or disciplining children was not common. Seventeenth-century French colonists often commented that Aboriginal parents loved their children so much they were unwilling to deny them anything.[24] The reality was more complex. Children were not indulged: they were taught their community responsibilities and trained in self-reliance and respect for others.[25] For example, an Inuit child who asked for consolation might be comforted, but one who was having a tantrum might be left to cry.[26]

Given that the Aboriginal education system was intertwined so tightly with both spiritual belief and daily life, it is not surprising that Aboriginal people were reluctant to give their children over to others to raise. In the early nineteenth century, the Ojibway in what is now Ontario made several efforts to integrate school-based education into their communities. Peter Jones, a man of European and Ojibway descent, played an important role in establishing day schools in communities in southern Ontario in the 1830s. In 1846 Ojibway leaders in southern Ontario

made a commitment to provide financial support for local residential schools.[27] Eventually, dissatisfaction with the schooling led many to drop their support.[28]

Others remained keenly interested in extending school to their communities. In 1871 Augustine Shingwauk, an Ojibway leader from Garden River, Ontario, travelled to Sarnia, London, and Toronto to seek the support of church leaders for a proposed "big teaching wigwam" for his community. There, he said, "children from the Great Chippeway Lake would be received and clothed, and fed, and taught how to read and how to write; and also how to farm and build houses, and make clothing; so that by and bye they might go back and teach their own people."[29] This initiative led to the establishment of the Shingwauk Home boarding school in 1873.

Aboriginal people on the Prairies had experience with mission schools that dated back to the 1820s. They recognized that education was necessary if they were to adjust to a changing economic and social situation, and insisted that schools, teachers, and salaries be included in the treaties negotiated in the 1870s. Government negotiator Alexander Morris assured them that "The Queen wishes her red children to learn the cunning of the white man and when they are ready for it she will send schoolmasters on every Reserve and pay them."[30] The early treaties called for on-reserve schools, and from Treaty Seven (1877) onward, the treaties committed the government to pay for teachers.[31] There was no mention of residential schools in the treaties or the negotiation process. Indeed, in one of his reports, Morris wrote: "The treaties provide for the establishment of schools, on the reserves, for the instruction of the Indian children. This is a very important feature, and is deserving of being pressed with the utmost energy."[32]

The Davin Report

In 1879 the federal government appointed Nicholas Flood Davin, an Irish-born, Toronto-based journalist, lawyer, and, most recently, an unsuccessful Conservative parliamentary candidate, to investigate the boarding school system in the United States with an eye to establishing similar schools in the North-West Territories. At the time of Davin's appointment, the United States was preparing to launch a new initiative: government-run, off-reservation manual training (or industrial) schools. These schools were to gather together youngsters from different reservations, separate them from their communities for

In 1879 Nicholas Flood Davin prepared a report recommending the Canadian government establish a series of residential schools for Aboriginal students in partnership with the churches. *Saskatchewan Archives Board, R-A6665.*

several years, and, it was hoped, provide them with skills that would allow them to earn a living. It was expected that students' attachments to their home communities would weaken while they were at school, and they would not return to their reservations upon graduation, thus contributing to breaking up reservations and tribes.[33]

Davin's investigation was not extensive; appointed on January 28, 1879, he submitted his report just forty-five days later, on March 14, 1879. During that time, he travelled to Washington, where he met with US government officials and representatives of a number of Native American nations.[34] He then made a brief visit to a mission school in Minnesota, and met with church and government officials in Manitoba. There, he also spoke with several Aboriginal people, whom he dismissed as chronic complainers.[35] He was disturbed to discover that since schools had been included in the treaties, Chief Prince, among a number of other chiefs, believed they "had some right to a voice regarding the character and management of the schools."[36] Davin said this would be a mistake, and that the schools were best kept out of the "designing predilections of a Chief."[37]

On the strength of his limited investigation, Davin recommended the federal government establish a partnership with the Canadian churches to operate four industrial schools on a residential basis in the Canadian West. By separating children from their parents and educating them in residential schools, Aboriginal children would be "gradually prepared to meet the necessities of the not distant future; to welcome and facilitate, it may be hoped, the settlement of the country."[38] Since there were, by Davin's estimate, 28,000 Indians and 1200 Métis families in the area covered by treaty, he warned that delay would be dangerous and expensive.[39]

Davin recommended a partnership with the churches for two reasons. The first was moral. The type of education he was advocating would undermine existing spiritual and cultural beliefs, and it would be wrong, he said, to destroy their faith "without supplying a better" one; namely, Christianity.[40] The second reason was economic. He said teachers should be paid adequately, but by hiring missionaries, the government would get "an enthusiastic person, with, therefore, a motive power beyond anything pecuniary remuneration could supply."[41] Put more plainly, dedicated religious men and women would be attracted to residential schools, even if the pay were substandard. This was an idea that, in coming years, the federal government would test to its limits.

To Civilize and Christianize

Government and church officials often said the role of the residential school was to civilize and Christianize Aboriginal children. When put into practice, these noble-sounding ambitions translated into an assault on Aboriginal culture, language, spiritual beliefs, and practices. Residential schools were seen as preferable to on-reserve day schools because they separated children from their parents, who were certain to oppose and resist such a radical cultural transformation.

The government's intent to break Aboriginal family bonds was clear from the outset. In 1887, Lawrence Vankoughnet, the deputy minister of Indian Affairs, justified the investment in residential schools by claiming that Aboriginal children who went to day schools "followed the terrible example set them by their parents."[42] The Archbishop of St. Boniface wrote in 1912 of the need to place Aboriginal children in residential schools at the age of six, since they had to be "caught young to be saved

The federal government supported not only the large industrial schools, but also smaller boarding schools, such as this Methodist school in Morley, Alberta, photographed in 1900. *David Ewens Collection, Library and Archives Canada, PA-182269.*

from what is on the whole the degenerating influence of their home environment."[43]

These schools were not just an assault on families. They were part of a larger government policy: the elimination of the economic and social responsibilities the government took on through the treaty process. At the heart of this policy was the *Indian Act*, which, in 1876, brought together all of Canada's legislation governing Indian people. The act both defined who Indians were under Canadian law and set out the process by which people would cease to be Indians. Under the act, the Canadian government assumed control of Indian peoples' governments, economy, religion, land, education, and even their personal lives. The act empowered the federal cabinet to depose chiefs and overturn band decisions—and the government used this authority to control band governments. Indian farmers could not sell their produce without the approval of the Indian agent, a government official responsible for the day-to-day enforcement of the act. Provisions in the *Indian Act* prohibited Indians from participating in sacred ceremonies such as the Potlatch on the west coast and the Sun Dance on the Prairies. Indians could not own reserve land as individuals, nor could they take advantage of the

homestead opportunities offered to other Canadians. The act placed new restrictions on Aboriginal hunting rights. The government had the power to move the bands if reserve land was needed by growing towns and cities. The government also gave itself increasing authority to lease or dispose of reserve land without band authorization. Under the act, it was illegal for Indians to possess alcohol or to patronize pool halls.

The act's ultimate goal was to bring Indian status to an end. This policy had been articulated first in the colonial government of Canada's 1857 *Act for the Gradual Civilization of the Indian Tribes in the Canadas*. Under this act, a male Indian (as defined by the government) in Ontario and Quebec who was fluent in either English or French, free of debt, and of good character could receive full citizenship, and fifty acres of reserve land and a share of band funds. Although this process was termed "enfranchisement," it did not actually provide the right to vote. Instead, it removed all distinctions between the legal rights and liabilities of Indians and those of other British subjects. Since an enfranchised person ceased to be an Indian in legal terms, the government expected that with

Deputy minister of Indian Affairs Duncan Campbell Scott said in 1920 that he was working for the day when "there is not a single Indian in Canada who has not been absorbed into the body politic."
Library and Archives Canada, Yousuf Karsh, Desiré Elise Scott collection, C-031512.

each enfranchisement, the number of Indians would decline, and the size of each reserve would shrink.

Two years after Confederation, the Canadian government adopted the *Act for the Gradual Enfranchisement of Indians*, which made enfranchisement the cornerstone of Canadian Indian policy. Enfranchisement was incorporated into the *Indian Act*.[44] From the outset, the policy was a failure; from 1859 to 1876, only one person was enfranchised voluntarily.[45] Since adult men were not interested in giving up their rights, government officials pinned their hopes on education.

The link between enfranchisement and residential schools was drawn clearly in 1920, when the government amended the *Indian Act* to allow it to enfranchise people without their consent, and to require school-aged Indian children to attend school. Duncan Campbell Scott, deputy minister of Indian Affairs, said the government would "continue until there is not a single Indian in Canada that has not been absorbed into the body politic, and there is no Indian question, and no Indian Department."[46] Residential schools were not established to meet the government's treaty obligations to provide schools (which were supposed to be on reserves), but to further its long-term aim of ending the country's treaty obligations by assimilating its Aboriginal population.

When it came to the educational purposes of the schools, government officials over the years expressed contradictory views. In 1889 Hayter Reed, Canada's Indian Commissioner for the Prairies, viewed the schools

as preparing people for the labour market. He said that "if the Indian is to become a source of profit to the country, it is clear he must be amalgamated with the white population."[47] While some industrial schools did provide training in printing and shoemaking, for the most part the vocational training in the schools was limited to farming and

> **"**
> *It is unlikely that any Tribe or tribes would give trouble of a serious nature to the Government whose members had children completely under Government control.*
> **"**
>
> Indian Affairs school inspector J.A. Macrae, 1886

associated skills such as blacksmithing and carpentry for boys and homemaking for girls. Teachers and tools were often in short supply. Deputy minister of Indian Affairs James Smart argued in 1898 that: "To educate children above the possibilities of their station, and create a distaste for what is certain to be their environment in life would be not only a waste of money but doing them an injury instead of conferring a benefit upon them."[48] At the same time, a future Indian Affairs minister, Frank Oliver, described government policy as either training Aboriginal people "to compete industrially with our own people, which seems to me a very undesirable use of public money, or else we are not able to educate them to compete, in which case our money is thrown away."[49] When the system was expanded in northern Canada in 1954, the federal government's Sub-Committee on Eskimo Education concluded: "The residential school is perhaps the most effective way of giving children from primitive environments, experience in education along the lines of civilization leading to vocational training to fit them for occupations in the white man's economy."[50]

Qu'Appelle school principal Father Joseph Hugonnard, staff, Grey Nuns, students, and parents in 1884, the year the school opened. *O.B. Buell, Library and Archives Canada, PA-118765.*

Safety and Security

There was a safety and security component to residential schools as well. One year after the 1885 Northwest Rebellion, Indian Affairs school inspector J.A. Macrae noted, "It is unlikely that any Tribe or tribes would give trouble of a serious nature to the Government whose members had children completely under Government control."[51] Duncan Campbell Scott worried in 1910 that "without education and with neglect the Indians would produce an undesirable and often dangerous element in society."[52]

Indeed, from the 1870s on, Canada had been sending other "dangerous elements"—the children of the urban poor—to industrial schools. Ontario's 1874 *Industrial Schools Act* allowed magistrates to commit neglected and truant children to industrial schools.[53] By 1900 there were four non-Aboriginal industrial schools in Ontario, two for girls and two for boys, with a total of 225 residents. Ten years later, there were also such schools in Nova Scotia, Quebec, Manitoba, and British Columbia.[54] In developing plans for a residential school in the Canadian northwest, Roman Catholic Bishop Vital Grandin drew on a visit he had made to a reformatory prison in Citeaux, France. The controlled and disciplined environment he observed there, coupled with the instruction in trades and the musical education the students received, seemed, in his view, to transform the young prisoners, and would do the same for Aboriginal children. Industry, economy, cleanliness, and sobriety were the prized virtues.[55]

The models for the residential schools, then, were not the private boarding schools established for the children of the young nation's elite, but reformatories and jails established for the children of the urban poor. Those institutions were judged to be failures by the early twentieth century, and largely abandoned, but the residential schools continued in operation.[56]

The Role of the Churches

As recommended by Davin, from 1883 onward the Canadian government was a major partner in the Canadian residential school system. Churches were eager to embrace the partnership because church missionary societies had laid the foundation for the system. For most of the system's history, the churches had responsibility for the day-to-day operation of the schools. Nineteenth-century missionaries believed their efforts to convert Aboriginal people to Christianity were part of a worldwide struggle for the salvation of souls. This belief provided justification for undermining traditional spiritual leaders (who were treated as agents of the devil), banning sacred cultural practices, and attempting to impose a new moral code on Aboriginal people by requiring them to abandon their traditional family structures. Individual missionaries often worked in isolation and under difficult conditions. Nevertheless, they were representatives of worldwide religious institutions that enjoyed the backing of influential elites in the most powerful nations of the world, including Canada.[57]

The two most prominent missionary organizations involved with residential schools in Canada in the nineteenth century were the Roman Catholic Oblates of Mary

An Oblate sister and child at the McIntosh School near Kenora, Ontario. *St. Boniface Historical Society Archives, Fonds Oblate Missionaries of the Sacred Heart and of Mary Immaculate, PA 821/9.*

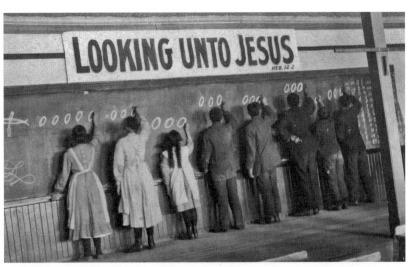

In his 1899 book *The Indians: Their Manner and Customs*, Methodist missionary John Maclean wrote that while the Canadian government wanted missionaries to "teach the Indians first to work and then to pray," the missionaries believed that their role was to "christianize first and then civilize." This photograph was taken at the Methodist school at Red Deer, Alberta, sometime between 1914 and 1919. *The United Church of Canada Archives, 93.049P850N.*

Immaculate and the Church Missionary Society of the Church of England (the Anglican Church). The Oblate order, founded in 1816 in southern France, was part of a broader Catholic response to the French Revolution. The Oblates emphasized the importance of unity, discipline, and the authority of the Pope, and enforced a strict moral code.[58] In the 1840s, Montreal Bishop Ignace Bourget invited the Oblates to Quebec. Soon, they were active not only in Quebec but also on the Prairies, in the North, and on the Pacific coast.[59] As a result of their dramatic expansion through the Canadian West and North, the Oblates established and managed the majority of church-run Canadian residential schools. This educational work would have been impossible without the support of a number of female religious orders, the prominent ones being the Sisters of Charity (also known as the Grey Nuns), the Sisters of Providence, the Sisters of St. Ann, and, in the twentieth century, the Oblate Sisters of Mary Immaculate. These female orders provided the school system with teachers and nurses. Although the Roman Catholic Jesuit order had a long history of missionary work among Aboriginal people in New France, in the nineteenth century, its work in residential schooling was limited to two schools on Manitoulin Island. These schools were relocated in the twentieth century to Spanish, Ontario.

The British-based Church Missionary Society was the first Anglican organization to focus solely on converting the "heathen" of the colonial world. It dispatched its first missionaries in 1802. In 1820 the Reverend John West

travelled on the society's behalf from England to Red River, where one of his first acts was to establish a residential school for Aboriginal children.[60] By 1901 the Church Missionary Society supported 510 male missionaries, 326 unmarried females, and 365 ordained indigenous pastors around the world.[61] Training in manual labour was to be an essential part of missionary schooling. As early as 1853, the head of the Church Missionary Society was able to report: "In India, New Zealand, and all our missions, an industrial department is being added to our schools."[62]

Methodist and Presbyterian mission societies, based in both Great Britain and the United States, also carried out work in Canada in the nineteenth century, and became involved in the operation of the residential school system. Women played a key role in the work of the Protestant missions. In some communities, residential schools grew out of the schools and orphanages that wives of missionaries established in their homes. Young women from Canada and Great Britain were recruited to work as nurses and teachers in remote northern schools, particularly in the early years of the system.[63]

Initially, the missionaries received considerable financial support from outside Canada. By the 1860s, the French branches of the Society for the Propagation of the Faith and the Society of the Holy Childhood were supporting forty-two Aboriginal children in four Oblate schools and two orphanages in western Canada.[64] The 1907 construction of the Church of England residential school at Chapleau, Ontario, was paid for with money raised in

In 1893 the federal government cut its funding for the High River school (pictured here in 1896) from $185.55 per student to $130 per student.
Canada. David Ewens Collection, Library and Archives Canada, PA-182268.

England.[65] To both Protestant and Catholic missionaries, Aboriginal spiritual beliefs were little more than superstition and witchcraft.[66] In British Columbia, William Duncan of the Church Missionary Society reported: "I cannot describe the conditions of this people better than by saying that it is just what might be expected in savage heathen life."[67] Missionaries led the campaign to outlaw Aboriginal sacred ceremonies such as the Potlatch on the west coast and the Sun Dance on the Prairies.[68] In British Columbia in 1884, for example, Roman Catholic missionaries argued for banning the Potlatch, saying that participation in the ceremony left many families so impoverished they had to withdraw their children from school to accompany them in the winter to help them search for food.[69]

While, on one front, missionaries were engaged in a war on Aboriginal culture, on another, they often served as advocates for protecting and advancing Aboriginal interests in their dealings with government and settlers. Many learned Aboriginal languages, and conducted religious ceremonies at the schools in those languages. These

efforts were not unrewarded: the 1899 census identified 70,000 of 100,000 Indian people in Canada as Christians.[70]

In the twentieth century, the Protestant churches established independent Canadian operations and missionary societies, and began to recruit their missionaries and school staff from within Canada. In 1925 the Methodist Church and the majority of Presbyterian congregations (along with the smaller Congregationalist Church) merged to create the United Church, which took over all the Methodist schools and many of the Presbyterian ones, as well.

The number of schools rose and fell throughout the system's history, but the Roman Catholic Church operated most of the schools, up to 60 percent of them at any one time. The Anglican Church operated about 25 percent of the schools, the United Church operated about 15 percent, and the Presbyterian Church ran only 2 or 3 percent of the schools. A United States-based Baptist church ran one school in the Yukon, and a Mennonite evangelical congregation operated three schools in northwestern Ontario. (A map showing school locations and religious affiliation is included at the back of this book.)

A group of students and parents from the Saddle Lake Reserve, en route to the Methodist-operated Red Deer, Alberta, school. *Woodruff. Department of Interior, Library and Archives Canada, PA-040715.*

While church and government officials would have their differences, their overall commitment to civilizing and Christianizing Aboriginal children gave rise to an education system that emphasized the need to separate children from their culture, impose a new set of values and beliefs, provide a basic elementary education, and implant Europe's emerging industrial work discipline.

The Rise of the System

From 1883 onward, the federal government began funding a growing number of industrial schools in the Canadian West. It also continued to provide regular funding to the church-run boarding schools. The residential system grew with the country. As Euro-Canadians settled the Prairies, British Columbia, and the North, increasing numbers of Aboriginal children were placed in residential schools.

As the system grew, controlling costs quickly became a primary concern for the federal government: salaries, for example, were reduced in 1888. By 1892 Ottawa was so concerned about rising industrial school costs that

it switched to a per-capita funding system under which churches were paid a set amount per student. With that money, school administrators were expected to pay for maintenance, salaries, and expenses. For the industrial schools, this new formula amounted to a cut in funding. At the High River, Alberta, school, for example, funding dropped from $185.55 per student to $130.00 a student.[71] This system also provided churches with an incentive to compete with one another in recruitment campaigns, and to enrol the maximum allowable number of students, even if they were in poor health or suffering from infectious disease.

The churches came to rely increasingly on student labour. This was provided through what was known as the "half-day system." Under this system, older students spent half the school day working. The fact that students spent only half their time in class guaranteed that most of them would receive an inferior education.[72]

By the beginning of the twentieth century, the federal government had concluded that industrial schools were poor investments. Many had been hastily built, were unhealthy, and had trouble attracting and keeping

File Hills, Saskatchewan, school, 1948. The half-day system, under which the students often spent half the day doing chores, ended only in 1951.
The United Church of Canada Archives, 93.049P1132N.

students. Indian Affairs minister Clifford Sifton concluded it would be better to close the industrial schools, and transfer the students and government support to smaller boarding schools.[73] Concern over the death rates in the residential schools gave rise to a movement within the Anglican Church to end the residential school system completely. In 1908 one of the leaders of this campaign, Samuel Blake, argued that the health conditions in the industrial schools were so dire that the government was leaving itself open to charges of manslaughter.[74] By 1908 federal Indian Affairs minister Frank Oliver had concluded that "the attempt to elevate the Indian by separating the child from his parents and educating him as a white man has turned out to be a deplorable failure."[75]

Despite such support in high places, the campaign to end the system failed in the face of opposition from the Catholic Church and some Protestant church leaders.[76] It did lead, in 1910, to a contract system that increased per-capita rates, and established a number of health guidelines. By then 3841 status Indian students were enrolled in seventy-four residential schools (the term that came to be applied to both industrial schools and boarding schools),

with another 6784 in 241 federally funded day schools. It was estimated that 45 percent of Indian children were not enrolled in school at all.[77] While the schools were intended only for children with status under the *Indian Act*, many Métis children attended these schools throughout the system's history. (For more on the Métis experience, see Chapter Four.)

The new funding system was only four years old when the First World War broke out. The war placed a financial strain on the federal government, and led it to abandon planned improvements and repairs to many residential schools.[78]

In 1920 the *Indian Act* was amended to make it compulsory for status Indian children between seven and fifteen to attend either day or residential school. In reality, between them the day schools and residential schools could accommodate little more than half the school-aged Indian children.[79]

Even with compulsory attendance laws in place, the schools had difficulty recruiting students. The principal of the Lejac school complained of having to spend his Septembers coaxing and threatening parents who were reluctant to send their children to school.[80] Over time, as enforcement of the attendance laws increased, in some locations Indian agents would show up in the fall and take children.[81] The churches sought and received court injunctions threatening parents with arrest if they did not bring their children to school.[82] In some cases, parents were jailed for refusing to do so.[83] Throughout the system's history, the government placed orphans or children it deemed to be delinquent or neglected into residential schools.

Parents also placed their children in the schools because they could not afford to care for them.[84] In some communities, parents, who were often former students themselves, reluctantly sent their children to school because it was the only educational opportunity available.[85]

Increases in school funding during the 1920s failed to keep pace with costs. The system suffered a fundamental breakdown in responsibility. Government officials often issued highly critical reports on the poor quality of food, harsh discipline, or overwork of students in a particular school. The churches had a standard response: to the degree that a problem existed, it could be resolved by an increase in funding. This generally brought the matter to an end. Indian Affairs regularly adopted various policies regarding health, discipline, and education, but these were not enforced consistently. At the outset, it had few school inspectors (and those it did have lacked educational qualifications). In later years, provincial school inspectors, who had no power to have their recommendations implemented, inspected the schools. From the record, it is clear that controlling costs was the prime policy objective. Having taken over the direction and funding of the church-run system in the 1880s, the federal government had enlarged the system without providing adequate funding or professional management. The schools could neither teach nor care for children.

By 1927 there were 77 residential schools with 6641 students.[86] In 1930 the Shubenacadie school, the only federally run school in the Maritimes, opened in Nova Scotia. It was intended for children who were orphans, deemed illegitimate, or neglected.[87] The first schools in Quebec, both at Fort George on James Bay (one Anglican, one Roman Catholic), opened in the early 1930s. In 1931 the system reached its peak number of schools, with eighty schools in operation.[88] However, even as the number of schools would decline in coming years, the number of students in attendance would increase.

The Great Depression of the 1930s led the federal government to cut funding repeatedly. The vulnerable suffered greatly during the Depression, but the children in residential schools shouldered far more than their share of the burden. In 1938, when the federal government was paying $180 per student for residential schools in Manitoba, the Manitoba School for the Deaf and the Manitoba School for Boys, both residential institutions, were receiving per-capita payments of $642 and $550, respectively, from the provincial government.[89] At the same time, the Children's Aid Society of Alberta estimated that the minimum cost of supporting a neglected child was a dollar a day, which, at $365 a year, was double what the federal government was spending per student in Manitoba residential schools.[90]

> **"**
>
> *...school integration represents the first step toward the dissolution of most reserves...*
>
> **"**
>
> The Hawthorn Report, 1967

The Long Decline

By the 1940s, the failure of the residential school system was apparent. The level of academic achievement was low. In 1930 only 3 percent of the students had gone beyond Grade 6. The comparable figure for the general Canadian school population was 33 percent.[91] By the end of the Second World War in 1945, the federal government was supporting less than eighty Aboriginal students at the high-school level.[92] Even though, for over twenty years, Indian Affairs supposedly had required that all teachers have provincial teaching certificates, a 1948 government study found that over 40 percent of staff had no professional training.[93] This was largely the legacy of underfunding. Because residential school teachers and staff were not paid competitive wages, it was particularly hard to hire skilled vocational education instructors, who could

These students are demonstrating in Edmonton in support of a 1970 campaign to have the Blue Quills, Alberta, school turned over to a First Nations educational authority. *Provincial Archives of Alberta, J48512.*

make far more money practising their trade than teaching it at a residential school.[94]

The federal government solution was not to work with parents to develop a more suitable education system. Instead, it simply decided to phase out residential schooling, and transfer First Nations education to the provinces. The first step in what turned out to be a lengthy process of closing the schools came in 1949, when the federal government agreed to pay a British Columbia school board to educate First Nations students. By the 1960s, it was negotiating similar agreements with provincial governments. This process was termed "integration," as opposed to "assimilation," but the old goals of enfranchisement remained. *The Hawthorn Report*, a 1967 government report on the status of First Nations people, concluded approvingly that "school integration represents the first step toward the dissolution of most reserves, because education makes it possible for the Indians to adapt themselves to the White Canadian's way of life."[95]

In 1951 the half-day system was ended officially, although many schools still depended heavily on student labour.[96] The per-capita system, with its incentive for overcrowding, remained in place until 1957.[97] The federal

government began hiring teachers directly in 1954. By 1962, 90 percent of the staff was fully qualified.[98]

The number of students in residential schools reached 10,000 in 1953.[99] Two years later, the Department of Northern Affairs and National Resources launched a major expansion of the system in northern Canada, building a series of schools and school residences, thus increasing the number of schools even as the government sought to close the schools in the South. (For more on the northern and Inuit experience, see Chapter Three.)

During the 1950s, the schools in southern Canada came to be used largely as child-welfare facilities. In 1953 almost 40 percent of the students in the schools had been placed there because the government had judged them to be neglected by their parents.[100] In 1966, on the eve of Canada's centennial celebrations, a federal study concluded that 75 percent of the students in the schools were from homes considered "unfit for school children."[101] The officials who made these decisions had little understanding of Aboriginal families or culture. Where children were at risk, governments did not provide any supports to help keep families together: they simply apprehended the children. This period of dramatically increased apprehension has become known as the "Sixties scoop," although it continued into the 1970s.[102]

Funding levels were not increased to reflect the fact that the schools were caring for children with a wide range of needs.[103] A 1967 study of residential schools in Saskatchewan found them to be crowded, poorly designed, and highly regimented. The study said this "absence of emphasis on the development of the individual child as a unique person is the most disturbing result of this whole system."[104]

Church involvement in the system was reduced dramatically in 1969, when the federal government took over the operation of most of the residential schools in the South. During this period, it also transferred responsibility for most of the northern schools and residences to the Yukon and Northwest Territories governments. Over the next decade, the government closed most of the schools, once more with little consultation with parents. When the government attempted to close the Blue Quills School near St. Paul, Alberta, the community protested. Parents and students did not want to see the school closed, they simply wanted it operated under local control. To block the closure, they occupied the school. As a result, Blue Quills, as well as a number of schools in Saskatchewan, British Columbia, and the North, continued to operate under the direction of First Nations educational authorities.[105] While the residential school system had largely wound down during the 1980s, the last residences (the Gordon's Student Residence and the Prince Albert Student Residence in Saskatchewan, and the Yellowknife, Inuvik, Cambridge Bay, and Iqaluit residences in the Northwest Territories) did not close until the mid-1990s.[106]

Just as the system was closing down, former students were speaking up. They began to mount an increasingly successful campaign to draw attention to the way they had been treated in the schools. That treatment is the essence of the residential school story. The next section of this book provides an overview of that experience from the first day through to the events that dominated daily life. It concludes with a discussion of an issue that has been in the public eye for much of the past decade: student abuse; and with one that has been largely ignored: the ways in which Aboriginal parents and children resisted the residential school system.

CHAPTER TWO

School Days: The Residential School Experience

Girls at the Gordon's school in Saskatchewan being transported to church by truck in 1953. *The General Synod Archives, Anglican Church of Canada, M2008-10 (P14).*

Arrival: "Now you are no longer an Indian."

In the 1940s, residential schools across the Canadian Prairies would send out battered trucks to collect students on the first day of school. The parents of children attending the Lestock school in Saskatchewan would bring their children to collection points, often the local farm instructor's office, where they would wait for the truck. According to George Peequaquat, "The size of the group increased as we went from reserve to reserve. It was not uncommon to have up to forty children ranging in age

from five to sixteen piled in the back of the truck."[1] In earlier decades, priests and ministers had brought students to school on wagon or by boat. In later years, they came by train or even plane. Few students ever forgot their first day at school.

On arrival, many students were overwhelmed by the sight of the residential school building. Simon Baker was excited by the imposing Lytton, British Columbia, school building.[2] Raphael Ironstand thought the Assiniboia school in Winnipeg "seemed enormous, with marbled floors and ceilings, and hallways about two hundred feet long. It smelled strongly of disinfectant, and our voices

Reverend Thompson Ferrier taking boys to school in Brandon, Manitoba, in 1904. The year before, the Methodist missionary James MacLachlan and six students he was taking from Berens River to the Brandon industrial school drowned in a canoe accident. *Manitoba Museum EP 347.*

echoed when we spoke. The whole place looked cold and sterile; even the walls were covered with pictures of stern-looking people in suits and stiff collars."[3] On her first sight of the Shingwauk school in Sault Ste. Marie, Ontario, Jane Willis thought, "Nothing could ever go wrong in such beautiful surroundings."[4] Originally impressed by the chapel at Shubenacadie, Isabelle Knockwood later concluded it was "a place where a lot of children's prayers did not get answered."[5]

When six-year-old Anthony Thrasher was deposited at the Roman Catholic school in Aklavik in the Northwest Territories, he saw the grey-habited nuns, heard their voices carried on the wind, and turned and ran. With no place to go, he was caught, grabbed by his hood, and dragged into the school, where he was scrubbed and checked for vermin, and put to bed.[6]

The assault on Aboriginal identity began the moment the child took the first step across the school's threshold. In 1893, at the age of six, Mike Mountain Horse was sent to the St. Paul's school on the Blood Reserve. "My Indian clothes, consisting of blanket, breech cloth, leggings, shirt and moccasins, were removed."[7] The embroidered parka and mukluks that Alice Blondin-Perrin's mother had made for her were taken on her arrival at school. She never saw them again.[8] Once stripped of their clothes, students were roughly bathed.[9]

Braided hair, which often had spiritual significance, was cut. At the Île-à-la-Crosse school in Saskatchewan, Alphonse Janvier was put on an old barber's chair. "I remember my head being shaved and all my long hair falling on the floor, and the way they dealt with my crying and the hurtful feeling was with a bowl of ice cream."[10]

Charlie Bigknife recalled being told, after his hair had been sheared off at the File Hills school in Saskatchewan, "Now you are no longer an Indian."[11] Students were given a new wardrobe—often used and ill-fitting.[12] Even though her grandmother had made her warm winter clothing, Lillian Elias was not allowed to wear it at the Roman Catholic school at Aklavik. Instead, all the students had to wear the same type of parka. "Maybe," she later wondered, "they wanted us to dress like them!"[13]

A new Christian identity required the imposition of new names. The first boy Anglican missionary John West recruited to his school at Red River in 1820, Pemutewithinew, became James Hope.[14] At the Aklavik Anglican school in the Northwest Territories, Masak became Alice—she would not hear her old name until she returned home.[15] Charles Nowell got his name "because a Sunday school teacher in England wanted Mr. Hall to give me his name, and they say that he was my godfather when I was baptized."[16] Jane Willis had been raised to answer to Janie Matthews, but on the residential school register at Fort George (now Chisasibi), Quebec, she was Janie Esquinimau, a nickname that belonged to her great-grandfather.[17] At the Qu'Appelle school in Saskatchewan, Ochankugahe (Path Maker) became Daniel Kennedy, named for the biblical Daniel, while Adélard Standing Buffalo was named for Adélard Langevin, the Archbishop of St. Boniface.[18]

Not only were children renamed, they were assigned numbers that corresponded to their clothes, their bed, and their locker. In some schools, they were expected to line up according to their numbers. "We were called by number all the time. The nuns used to call, '39, 3 where

Girls at the Shingwauk school in Sault Ste. Marie, dressed for church in 1941. The federal government and the churches used posed photographs to promote the residential school system across Canada. The image that they give of life at the schools was not always accurate. For example, in 1936, a government inspector noted that at the Birtle, Manitoba, school "all the children have good clothes but these are kept for Sundays and when the children go downtown—in other words when out where they can be seen, they are well dressed." *The General Synod Archives, Anglican Church of Canada, P2004-09 (63).*

are you?' or '25, come here right now!'"[19] A student who attended the St.-Marc-de-Figuery school in Amos, Quebec, felt stripped of her identity: "I was number one hundred and sixteen. I was trying to find myself; I was lost. I felt like I had been placed in a black garbage bag that was sealed. Everything was black, completely black to my eyes and I wondered if I was the only one to feel that way."[20]

Boys and girls were strictly segregated. After the first day of classes, Raphael Ironstand did not see his sister for the rest of the year. "I still remember her looking apprehensively over her shoulder as she was led away."[21] At dinnertime on her first day at the Anglican school at Aklavik, Alice French, seeing her brother looking lost and lonesome, started over to comfort him, only to be put back into line. During the years they spent at the school, they rarely spoke, only shouting out to one another at mealtime, or on the schoolyard or in the dining hall.[22]

A girl from the Kamloops school recalled, "I remember seeing my brother in the back of the class. I went to talk to him and he was really nervous. He said, 'Don't come

over and talk to me.' I asked, 'Why, I want to talk to you.' And he was saying, 'You're not supposed to.' I told him. 'Why, you are my brother.' And right away I was taken to the front of the class and I was given the ruler on the palm of my hands."[23]

Student life was highly regimented and disciplined. "During certain periods of the day we were not allowed to talk, which only led to hand motions and sneaking around in secrecy."[24] Inez Deiter, who attended the Onion Lake school in Saskatchewan in the 1930s, recalled, "We used to have to use this sign language to communicate."[25] A girl from Fort Hope, in northern Ontario, recalled that in the 1970s, "there seemed to be bells everywhere. There was the morning bell at seven, when a nun came into our dormitory clapping her hands. She would make us say prayers, like Deo Gratias, on our knees beside our beds. Then there was a bell for breakfast, one for classes at nine, one for ten when we would play outside, one for lunch, and others too. The nun in my class also had a small bell that she rang to signal us when we should stand up and sit down."[26]

Students outside the school in Shingle Point, Yukon, in approximately 1930. *The General Synod Archives, Anglican Church of Canada, P9901-570.*

At the Shubenacadie school in Nova Scotia, Rita Joe was told "when to go to the bathroom, when to eat, when to do this and that, when to pray. We were even told when to yawn and cough. Children can't help themselves when they cough, but we were told, 'Stop your barking!'"[27] The feeling of being under constant surveillance continued for years. It was, former Spanish, Ontario, student Basil Johnston concluded, the sort of treatment that would be given to felons.[28]

Children were crushed by loneliness. A note in the 1888 High River school journal said that since he had been enrolled in the school, Lawrence Faber "has done nothing in school for the last few months and cries nearly every day."[29] On arrival at the Onion Lake school, Elise Charland had to deal with both her own loneliness and that of her younger brother. "There was no one there to help us, to love us, to take us in their arms and take the hurt and tears away. That loneliness was unbearable. No one cared whether we lived or died."[30] Former Beauval, Saskatchewan, student Maria Campbell could recall "little from that part of my life besides feeling lonely and frightened when I was left with the Sister at the school."[31] Another former student said, "Little kids used to be home-sick for their homes. Oh, yes, they used to cry at night."[32] Millicent Stonechild felt that living at File Hills was the same as being sent to Siberia. "We were so totally isolated in this boarding school. All around the schoolyard, there

were fences, beyond which we didn't set foot. Bells were ringing all day long."[33]

Different schools had different policies for family visits. Some had family rooms or porches where parents could visit their children on weekends. Some parents or grandparents were able to take their children on picnics. However, in other cases, distances were too great, travel costs too high, and school policy too forbidding for parents to have any contact with their children. In 1919 Edward Elliot travelled to Kuper Island, British Columbia, to see his son. "When I got there I could not see my boy and the priest who was the principal would have nothing to do with me."[34] Ralph Sandy went to the Kamloops school in the 1940s. To him, "That was the saddest part of all, missing your moms and dads. You don't see them, maybe, ten months at a time."[35] Letters home—or to anyone else—were read and often censored by teachers.[36]

The Indian Affairs program of studies of 1896 stated: "Every effort must be made to induce pupils to speak English and to teach them to understand it; unless they do, the whole work of the teacher is likely to be wasted."[37] The schools had differing language policies over the years, but the message most children received was 'don't speak your own language.' "If we were heard speaking Shuswap, we were punished. We were made to write on the board one hundred times, 'I will not speak Indian any more.'"[38] At Shubenacadie, "The most enduring and unyielding

A mother bringing her children to the St. John's School in Wabasca, Alberta, in the 1920s. *The General Synod Archives, Anglican Church of Canada, P75-103 (S8-242).*

law was the one that forbade the speaking of Mi'kmaw even during play."[39] At the St.-Marc-de-Figuery school in Amos, Quebec, which did not open until 1955, French was the language of instruction. One former student recalled being "forbidden from speaking to my sisters and we were prohibited from speaking our language."[40]

For some, school was exciting, the clothing novel, and the food an improvement, but for most students, residential school was an alien and frightening experience. Loneliness and hunger were constants. While many former students point to a teacher who took an interest in them, helping them learn, develop a skill, or excel at a sport, the reality is that, in most schools, there were too few teachers and too many responsibilities. Children rebelled or withdrew into themselves. The schools responded with more rules and more discipline.

Mary John's recollection of the Lejac school captures the atmosphere that would have been familiar to many students: "Within the school itself, the missionaries and the nuns had to deal with one hundred and eighty Native children who were always hungry, always homesick. The

boys were openly rebellious, many of them stealing or running away or getting the girls off in some corner alone with them. Unlike the boys, the female students were seldom openly rebellious. Instead they were sullen and depressed."[41]

Education: "Lots of copying and memorizing."

From the outset, the government's educational expectations for residential schools were not high. In 1889 Hayter Reed, a future deputy minister of Indian Affairs, wrote that residential school children should not be educated to "earn their bread by brain-work rather than by manual labour."[42] Fifteen years later, Clifford Sifton, the minister of Indian Affairs, asserted that "the Indian cannot go out from school, making his own way and compete with the white man.... He has not the physical, mental or moral get-up to enable him to compete."[43] In 1917 an Indian Affairs official questioned whether the Fort Providence school in the North-West Territories was giving students too much education. How much time, he wondered, was needed to give children "sufficient education to fear God, honour the King, and respect the laws of the country."[44]

Although students sometimes attended the schools until well into their teens, it was not until after the Second World War that the schools began to offer courses at the high-school level. In 1960 the percentage of First Nations students—in any type of school—who went beyond Grade 6 had increased from 3 percent in 1930 to 22 percent. The average for the non-Aboriginal population was 37 percent.[45] Into the 1960s, the people who ran the system still saw their goal as overseeing the assimilation of Aboriginal people, who were viewed as being adrift "in a sea of cultural transition."[46] Nor was there any meaningful Aboriginal curriculum: in 1965 the government acknowledged that any reference to Indians in its curriculum had been either romantic or misleading.[47]

The Lejac, British Columbia, school was typical of many in the system. Classes were large—between forty and fifty students—and included students of all ages. Given these constraints, teachers fell back on recitation and drill. Memorization and parroting the "right" answer were staples of this approach. The school lacked readers, textbooks, and a library.[48] Florence Bird's education at Holy Angels at Fort Chipewyan in the first decade of the

Sister McQuillan and students at the Fort Resolution, Northwest Territories, school in 1923. *Hudson's Bay Company Archives, Archives of Manitoba, 1987/363-I-47.1/1 (N60-2).*

twentieth century was similar: "School in my time was mostly memorizing, not much teaching and talking. Lots of copying and memorizing. The sisters were not really teachers but they did their best."[49]

At Shubenacadie, according to Isabelle Knockwood, during tests, "everyone sat at their desks with folded hands." Individual students were asked questions that "they answered according to the book. Written tests or exams were never given."[50] Of her early education at Kamloops, Pauline Arnouse said, "When we couldn't get our additions and subtractions right, I remember her using the whip on our knuckles. I remember my knuckles being black and blue and sore."[51] At that school, a frustrated Ron Ignace found that the harder he studied, the less he learned. "I remember even going to the priest and saying, 'Look father, I really want to learn but my grades are getting worse, and worse, and worse. I don't know what to do.'"[52]

George Raley, the principal of the Coqualeetza, British Columbia, school, emphasized academic achievement, ensuring that even under the half-day system, students completed a grade a year. His was the first school to offer Grade 9 on the full-day model. When the government closed the Coqualeetza school in 1940, many staff believed the measure was taken because of Raley's commitment to Aboriginal education.[53]

The system attracted many idealistic and hard-working teachers. Nevertheless, Indian Affairs officials were aware that during much of the system's history, many of the teachers would not have been able to get jobs in the regular school system, and that the churches assigned to residential schools people who, as one federal official put it, "have not been too successful in other fields of activity."[54]

For many of the most committed teachers, religion was the fourth "R," and of greater importance than reading, writing, or arithmetic. According to Janice Acoose, the daily routine at Cowessess, Saskatchewan, in the 1950s was "early rise, prayers, shower and dress, meals premised by prayers, school premised by more prayers, rigidly programmed exercise time, catechism instruction and bedtime, which was premised by excruciatingly painful periods of time spent on our knees in prayer circles."[55] Solomon Pooyak observed, "All we ever got was religion, religion, religion. I can still fall on my knees at seventy-two years of age and not hurt myself because of the training and conditioning I got at Delmas."[56] A former Kamloops student, Cedric Duncan, had a similar memory: "Seemed like they just wanted us to learn about praying and all that

The message on the blackboard of this Anglican-run school in Lac la Ronge, Saskatchewan, in 1945 is "Thou Shalt Not Tell Lies." *Bud Glunz, National Film Board of Canada, Photothèque, Library and Archives Canada, PA-134110.*

stuff quite a bit. They didn't really care about our school-work, you know and help us with that."[57] In 1912 a federal government Indian agent wrote that teachers tended "to devote too much time to imparting religious instruction to the children as compared with the imparting of secular knowledge."[58] Attracting and keeping good teachers was an ongoing problem throughout the system's history. At one point, when public school teachers in the West were earning between $500 and $650 a year, Indian Affairs was allowing residential schools $300 a year for teach-ers.[59] In the 1950s, the federal government began hiring and paying teachers directly, leading to long-needed sal-ary improvements.

Aside from the low pay, the workloads in the schools were staggering. In the 1920s at Mount Elgin, there were two teachers and 148 students.[60] Sixty years later, the work-day of a childcare worker at the Prince Albert school, who was responsible for twenty-four girls ranging in age from six to sixteen, started at 6:45 in the morning when she

prepared lunch for a girl who was returning home for a funeral. Over the next hour, she woke the rest of the girls, supervised their breakfast, and ensured they took appro-priate medications. By 9:00 she had to get the girls dressed and ready for school, while fitting in a conversation with two girls who had not been attending scheduled Al-a-teen meetings. With just three and a half hours of break scattered throughout the schedule, her workday, which would include two more meals, and the supervision of a study period and of playtime, did not end until the 10:00 p.m. bedtime of the oldest girls.[61] In the system's early days, many staff worked year-round without a day off.[62]

Richard King, who taught at the Choutla school in the Yukon during the 1962–1963 school year, concluded that the school's record-keeping system "would be unaccept-able in any well-run stock farm, where at the very least, parentage, production records, and performance charac-teristics of each animal are minimal records to be main-tained." In the case of one sixteen-year-old girl, who had

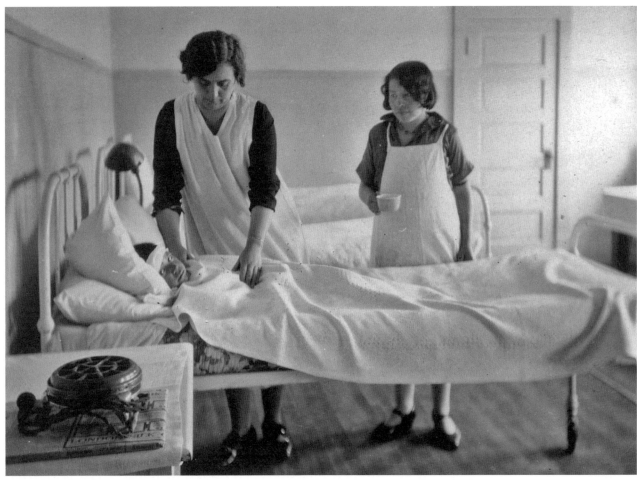

Sick student at the Edmonton school (sometime between 1925 to 1935). *The United Church of Canada Archives, 93.049P870N.*

been at the school for eight years and was still only in the fourth grade, her school record consisted of a single page of test scores.[63] As Bernard Pinay philosophically summed up his educational experience, "I have nothing against File Hills School. The only thing is I didn't get much schooling because I spent a lot of time working on the farm." [64]

Health: "My kingdom for a nurse."

During the period the residential schools were in operation, no matter how bad health conditions were for the general Canadian population, they were worse for Aboriginal Canadians. From the outset, death rates at residential schools were high. In the Qu'Appelle school's first decade of operation, 174 students (out of a total enrolment of 344) were, to use the school's term, "discharged." More than half these students died either at the school or shortly after being sent home. In 1887 the Battleford school, down to an enrolment of fifteen, lost two children to spinal meningitis.[65] In 1909, nearly all the High River school's sixty students were diagnosed with tuberculosis.[66]

Seven years later, an entry in the school's journal plaintively read, "A nurse! A nurse! My kingdom for a nurse."[67] A 1900 report showed that twelve of sixty-six former students of the Red Deer school were dead. Three years later, six students at the school died of tuberculosis.[68]

Disrupting a people's relationship with the environment, and increasing their stress levels, can leave them susceptible to illness and epidemic. In the 1880s, the Canadian government altered the Aboriginal relationship to the environment in western Canada in two profound ways. First, people who had long been hunters were confined to reserves where they were expected to become peasant farmers. Reserve housing was poor and crowded, sanitation inadequate, and access to clean water limited. Second, many of their children were placed in crowded, poorly ventilated residential schools. In these schools, students were subjected to the intense stress of separation from their families, and the requirement to learn a new language and new culture. The result was tragic: from the 1880s until well into the twentieth century, smallpox, measles, influenza, dysentery, and tuberculosis cut a trail of death and suffering through western Canadian Aboriginal communities.[69]

This trail led to the schools. In 1907 Dr. Peter Bryce, the chief medical officer for Indian Affairs, published a damning report on the health conditions at boarding and residential schools on the Prairies. He was particularly alarmed by the poor air circulation in the thirty-five schools he inspected: "with but two or three exceptions no serious attempt at the ventilation of dormitories or school-rooms has hitherto been made; that the air-space of both is, in the absence of regular and sufficient ventilation, extremely inadequate; that for at least 7 months in the long winter of the west, double sashes are on the windows in order to save fuel and maintain warmth and that for some 10 continuous hours children are confined in dormitories, the air of which, if pure to start with, has within 15 minutes become polluted...."[70]

Bryce asked the principals to conduct surveys on the health of former students. Only fifteen of the thirty-five principals submitted the requested information, but the results painted a devastating picture. According to their reports, between 1888 and 1905, 1537 students had been admitted to their schools. Bryce reported that of this enrolment, "nearly 25 per cent are dead, of one school with an absolutely accurate statement, 69 percent of ex-pupils are dead, and that everywhere the almost invariable cause of death given is tuberculosis."[71] Aside from the poor condition of the schools, Bryce was alarmed by the high number of sick children being admitted to the schools, where disease, particularly tuberculosis, could spread quickly to virtually every student.

A 1909 follow-up study of prairie schools was just as worrisome: two schools in Alberta, Old Sun and Peigan, had death rates of 47 percent.[72] Similar studies were not carried out in British Columbia or Ontario, but problems existed there as well. From 1896 to 1904, as many as twenty-five children a year were on sick leave at the Kuper Island school in British Columbia, which had a maximum enrolment of fifty-eight. By 1905 fifty-five of the Coqualeetza school's 269 former students were dead.[73] In 1908 seven of the thirty-one children attending the Chapleau school in northern Ontario died in a three-month period, making it all but impossible for the school to recruit new students.[74]

Bryce recommended that he be given control over certain schools, and that there be a significant improvement in the care given to sick students.[75] Duncan Campbell Scott, the Indian Affairs superintendent of education, said the plan was not realistic.[76] Instead of implementing Bryce's recommendations, Indian Affairs reached an agreement with the churches in 1910 to increase funding, set standards for diet and ventilation, and ensure that sick children were not admitted.[77] In 1913 Scott, by then the deputy minister of Indian Affairs, acknowledged in a review of the department's first forty-five years that "It is quite within the mark to say that fifty per cent of the children who passed through these schools did not live to benefit from the education which they had received therein."[78] Yet, shortly after assuming his duties as deputy minister, Scott forced Bryce out of office, and, in 1918, to save money, he eliminated the position of medical inspector, leaving the department completely unprepared for that year's deadly influenza epidemic.[79]

> "
> *...fifty per cent of the children who passed through these schools did not live to benefit from the education which they had received therein.*
> "
>
> Deputy minister of Indian Affairs, Duncan Campbell Scott, 1913

The 1918–1919 Spanish flu epidemic killed 30,000 Canadians, 4000 of whom were Aboriginal.[80] Residential schools were hit particularly hard. At the Red Deer school, virtually all the staff and students fell ill, and five students died. According to the school principal, the lack of resources for dealing with the epidemic was "nothing less than criminal."[81] To cut costs, the children were buried two to a grave.[82] At the High River school, where the entire school was struck down, the principal and three students died.[83] In British Columbia, all the students at the Coqualeetza, Kitamaat, and St. Mary's schools came down with the flu.[84] Similar tales could be told of most other schools.

In his 1907 report on health conditions in residential schools, Dr. Peter Bryce noted that the Red Deer, Alberta, school had the worst mortality rate of the industrial schools he had examined. In the 1906-07 school year, six children died at the school. These sorts of results led Bryce to title his 1922 booklet on Aboriginal health in Canada *The Story of a National Crime*. *The United Church of Canada Archives, 93.049P843N. (19--?)*

Although the death rates fell in the following years, there are no clear records as to how many children died while attending residential schools, and the total may reach into the thousands.[85] As at Red Deer, many children were buried in school cemeteries. In some cases, parents never were told what had become of their children. The memoirs of former residential school students are filled with remembrances of death and disease. In the late 1870s, Charles Nowell watched a girl he had fallen in love with die of whooping cough at the Alert Bay school.[86] In the 1920s, Edward Ahenakew wrote, "Again and again I have seen children come home from boarding schools only to die, having lost during their time at school all the natural joys of the association with their own families, victims of an educational policy, well-meant but not over-wise."[87]

Eleanor Brass attributed the death of one of her brothers in the early twentieth century at the File Hills, Saskatchewan, school to neglect.[88] Earl Maquinna George, who attended the Ahousaht school in British Columbia in the 1930s, recalled "a time when the school had a measles epidemic, and the whole 200 kids except one, a teenage girl, were put to bed. Miss Reed and this one young girl together looked after all the 200 kids who were in sick bay."[89] In the 1940s, every student and staff member at the St. Phillip's Anglican school on James Bay was stricken with influenza. Jane Willis recalled: "The older girls were dragged out of bed every day to prepare the meals and wash the dishes, then sent back to bed as soon as they had completed their work."[90] As late as 1959, crowded conditions at Stringer Hall, the Anglican residence in Inuvik, caused an outbreak of measles to spread quickly through the dormitories.[91]

Aboriginal health care was never a priority. Tuberculosis among Aboriginal people largely was ignored until it threatened the general population.[92] In 1937 Dr. H.W. McGill, the director of Indian Affairs, sent out an instruction that Indian health-care services "must be restricted to those required for the safety of limb, life or essential function." Hospital care was to be limited, spending on drugs cut in half, and sanatoria and hospital treatment for chronic tuberculosis eliminated.[93] Not until the 1940s was there an improvement in government medical services to Aboriginal people.[94]

Chronic underfunding and overcrowding undermined the health of students attending residential schools. School principals, doctors, and Indian Affairs officials regularly ignored regulations prohibiting the admission of infected children. Inspections were limited and irregular, and violations of regulations regarding overcrowding and poor diet rarely were addressed properly. All these circumstances contributed to the spread of infectious illnesses and diseases.[95] Aboriginal children, who were supposed to be protected by the Canadian government, were, in fact, underfed, poorly housed, and overworked, for decades.

The Qu'Appelle, Saskatchewan, school dining room in 1900. In 1891, when the government accused the churches of spending too much on food, Qu'Appelle school principal Father Joseph Hugonnard responded that, at the end of a meal, students would complain "they had not had enough to eat and upon enquiry have found that it was never without good reason." *St. Boniface Historical Society Archives: Father Joseph Hugonard, Oblates of Mary Immaculate Fonds, SHSB 23107.*

Hunger: "The first and the last thing I can remember."

Frederick Loft, who went on to establish the League of Indians of Canada, one of the first Canadian Aboriginal political organizations, attended the Mohawk Institute in Brantford, Ontario, in 1873. Many years later, he wrote, "I recall the times when working in the fields, I was actually too hungry to be able to walk, let alone work."[96] Fifty years later, George Manuel, who eventually helped found the National Indian Brotherhood and the World Council of Indigenous Peoples, attended the Kamloops school. Of his time there, he wrote, "Hunger is both the first and the last thing I can remember about that school.… Every Indian student smelled of hunger."[97] It was a problem that refused to go away. Mabel James, a student at the St. Michael's school at Alert Bay, British Columbia, from 1951

to 1959, was haunted by the same memories as Frederick Loft and George Manuel. "I always felt hungry. We didn't get big helpings of food. There wasn't much variety."[98]

Pauline Creeley recalled that at File Hills, "We were hungry all the time." Porridge with skim milk was the standard breakfast. "At dinnertime, we'd have some kind of mush, a stew of some sort, a pudding and a slice of bread, no butter. At suppertime, we'd have the same kind of mush, some vegetables.[99] Magee Shaw's memories of breakfast at Saskatchewan's St. Bernard school were of "porridge, no milk, no sugar and you were always sitting in silence in a big room."[100] Theresa Meltenberger, who spent five years at Lac la Biche in the 1930s and 1940s, recalled, "The mainstay of our diet was a porridge which was actually cracked wheat that sat on the back of the stove all night, ended up with a bunch of lumps and kind of slimy. I couldn't swallow it, so for the most part my

The dining room of the Edmonton residential school (sometime between 1925 and 1936). *The United Church of Canada Archives, 93.049P871N.*

mornings were spent in front of my bowl of porridge—to this day I can't look porridge in the face."[101]

Beans were such a staple of residential school meals that some Métis students in Alberta found themselves being labelled "mission beans."[102] Geraldine Schroeder remembered that at Kamloops, the younger students cleaned the dry beans and sometimes did not remove all the stones. "You know how you're eating and all of sudden you'd bite down on a rock and it would crack a tooth."[103]

Not only were they hungry, many students had difficulty adjusting to a diet that was different from what they were used to at home. At Lejac, Mary John "missed the roast moose, the dried beaver meat, the fish fresh from a frying pan, the warm bread and bannock and berries. Oh, how I missed the food I used to have in my own home."[104] The children coming to residential school had little exposure to cooked vegetables, macaroni, eggs, cheese, or processed meats. As a student at the Roman Catholic school at Aklavik, six-year-old Anthony Thrasher was not used to cooked food, and, along with other boys, would sneak into the kitchen to steal frozen meat to eat. When one of the nuns realized that the boys liked raw frozen meat, she used to give it to them as treats.[105]

Peter Irniq (who became the Commissioner of Nunavut), originally from Repulse Bay (now Naujaat), recalled the food at Turquetil Hall in Chesterfield Inlet on Hudson Bay as "terrible." Although school staff served

Arctic char, "they left the guts in the artic char so that food just tasted horrible. And yet we had to eat it. We had no other choice but to eat the arctic char with guts."[106]

At the Fort Alexander school in Manitoba, Phil Fontaine, the future National Chief of the Assembly of First Nations, often refused to eat. "As a result of that I started being called 'King'. King was something that wasn't acceptable in there. If kids didn't like the food it was thrown on the floor. I was forced to eat off the floor a couple of times and the kids were told to watch the King eat, so the King ate. I felt horrible and humiliated. Eating became a real psychological terror."[107]

The residential schools were meant to be self-supporting. For much of their history, the older boys at the schools spent a good part of each day farming. In some cases, the land was poor, the weather was bad, and the boys simply too young to farm successfully. But in other cases, to raise money, the schools sold a portion of the food the students had raised. At the Lytton school in British Columbia, butter from the creamery was sold with the vegetables and fruit the school farm produced, and at Carcross school, milk and eggs were sold to the local community.[108] In many schools, milk was separated and the cream was sold, leaving the students to drink the skimmed milk. One government inspector thought student health would be improved by simply banning cream

Staff and students making butter at the Old Sun School in Alberta, in 1945. *The General Synod Archives, Anglican Church of Canada, P7538 (1006).*

separators from the schools and allowing the children to drink whole milk.[109]

Not surprisingly, students began to fend for themselves. At prairie schools such as File Hills, the boys would trap gophers and roast them over open fires to supplement their diets, occasionally sharing these treats with the girls.[110] At the Anglican school at Aklavik, students were given musk-rat traps. They were allowed to keep the money they raised from selling the furs, while the meat was served, roasted, at the school.[111] Kamloops was one of the schools where students supplemented their diets with dandelion roots, rose-buds, and green leaves. These were acts of desperation, not a return to traditional diets.[112] If they were burning weeds and leaves, students might throw a few potatoes in the bonfire on the sly, in hopes of getting a half-cooked potato when the fire burned down.[113] At the United Church school in Edmonton, prairie boys taught Art Collison, who was from British Columbia, to hunt with homemade slingshots. "When we were hungry we would hunt for rabbits and later roast them over an open fire before eating them. We also boiled the rabbits and porcupine in a one-gallon pail on an open fire and this was our Indian treat."[114]

For many students, the only memories they have of being well fed are associated with visits from their parents. Isabelle Knockwood, at the Shubenacadie school in Nova Scotia, recalled the relief she felt "every Sunday when Mom and Dad came to see us and brought food—mostly home-made blueberry pies—and we'd get to be a family for an hour."[115] At Christmas and Easter, George Manuel's grandparents would visit, bringing "deer meat and ban-nock and other real food you could get full on."[116]

Memories of illicitly taking food from the kitchen, the storeroom, or the garden run through residential school memoirs. In the 1910s, File Hill students discovered bar-rels of apples in the school attic that were meant for the staff. Over time, the students worked their way through the barrel. When the deed was discovered, the students were strapped and sent to bed without a meal.[117] William Brewer could recall risking a strapping by going down to the root cellar to take apples at Kamloops. "They were good. When you're hungry, anything's good."[118] Ralph Sandy echoed this sentiment: "In order to survive in that school we had to learn how to steal, too. If you didn't steal, boy I'm telling you, you'd starve."[119] In the 1960s, a group of older boys began to take food from the kitchen and distribute it to other students at the Kamloops school. According to a former Kamloops student, "We would break into that kitchen and lock it up the same way we broke in. We would get oranges, apples, and all these other goodies. We would sneak down to those kids, give them an apple and tell them to eat everything right to the core."[120] Even at far northern Aklavik, the principal kept a vegetable garden the students would raid, at the risk of a spanking.[121]

The Elkhorn, Manitoba, school kitchen staff in the 1930s. *The General Synod Archives, Anglican Church of Canada, P7538 (902).*

In 1904 an Indian Affairs study showed that students at the Regina school were not being fed according to the government's allowance, while the principal was buying luxury foods including sardines, lemons, oranges, chocolates, and canned salmon.[122] Although most staff did not eat luxury food, many students recalled that the staff was better fed than the students. John PeeAce, a former student at the Lestock school in Saskatchewan, remembered "walking past the staff dining room and noticing that they were having steak and chicken. It looked like a king's feast. We had baloney sandwiches."[123]

The quality of the food improved when outside inspectors and other visitors were present. A Métis student from Alberta recalled, "The welfare was coming this one time, they used to put tablecloths on the table and give us bacon and eggs to make it look like it was really good food, you know."[124] In his memoir of his days at the boys' school in Spanish, Ontario, Basil Johnston wrote of how, in the presence of outside inspectors, the boys got butter rather than lard, the soup seemed thicker, and boiled eggs accompanied the mush. When they explained to the inspectors that this was not their regular fare, they were not believed.[125]

At the 1902 inquest into the case of a boy who froze to death after running away from the Williams Lake, British Columbia, school, several students testified they had run away because the food at the school was poor. Ellen Charlie described the food as being "fit only for pigs, the meat was rotten, and had a bad smell and taste."[126]

According to Christine Haines, "they gave me rotten food to eat and punished me for not eating it—the meat and soup were rotten and tasted so bad they made the girls sick."[127] The dead boy's father said his son had run away the previous year because "he did not get sufficient food and that they whipped him too much."[128]

These are not just childhood memories of children sick for home and their mothers' cooking. Dietary studies carried out by agencies such as the Red Cross in the 1940s confirm the students' recollections.[129] Furthermore, the inadequate quality and amount of food available at the residential schools was an acknowledged problem from the very beginning. In 1897 Indian Affairs official Martin Benson described the food at one school as "monotonous,"[130] and fifty years later, another inspector, A. McCready, found the food at eight schools inadequate in both quantity and quality.[131] In 1918 an Indian agent, J. Smith, described the meal at the Kamloops school as "very slim for growing boys."[132] The government not only was aware of the problems, it was aware of their continuity. A 1945 nutritional study of the Spanish, Ontario, school commented on the "unusually large quantities of beans which they consumed every other day."[133] During the 1940s, the Canadian Red Cross conducted a number of surveys of food quality at the residential schools, and concluded the food at the Chapleau school in northern Ontario was "distinctly unpalatable,"[134] while at Mount Elgin, meals were "simply appalling."[135] In 1956 limited rations at the Moose Fort school in northern Ontario had

Students at All Saints School in Lac la Ronge, Saskatchewan, carrying wood in the 1920s. *The General Synod Archives, Anglican Church of Canada, P7538 (231).*

led to embarrassing reports of children scavenging for food in garbage cans.[136]

Some students had more positive memories. Edna Gregoire, who went to the Kamloops school in the 1930s, said "the food was nice, we had home-baked bread, and they would make toast out of it, and they had cereal in the morning with nice fresh milk, because they had milk cows there. So I was happy with the food."[137] At times, improvements were made. In Alice Blondin-Perrin's opinion, the meals improved dramatically when the students were transferred from the dilapidated St. Joseph's school at Fort Resolution to the brand-new Breynat Hall at Fort Smith in the Northwest Territories in 1957. "The dinners were always delicious, with mashed potatoes, meat, meatloaf, or fish, and vegetables. I could now eat cooked carrots, beets, turnips, and peas which I used to hate the taste of, but now loved."[138] In the 1970s, Nathan Matthew, a Secwepemc (Shuswap) man, became a senior administrator of the Kamloops residence, and initiated what former students recalled as a "revolution" in the dining hall. According to Eddy Jules, "In three days he changed that place just like you would snap your fingers. We were having waffles and boiled eggs, bacon and eggs, you name it. We thought we had just died and went to heaven. Milk was real milk, you know. It was wild, it was totally wild, he was a godsend. To this day I have so much respect for that man."[139]

Work: "Worked too hard and taught too little."

For most of their history, residential schools depended on student labour to survive. Until the 1950s, the schools ran on what was called the "half-day system." Under this system, the older students spent half a day in class, while the other half was supposed to be spent in vocational training. In reality, this training often simply amounted to free labour for the school. The girls prepared the meals, did the cleaning, and made and repaired much of the student clothing. The boys farmed, raised animals, did repairs, ran tailor shops, and made and repaired shoes. In many cases, the students were not learning, but performing the same laborious tasks again and again.

Government inspectors were well aware of this problem. An 1893 report on the Rupert's Land school in Middlechurch, Manitoba, describes the students as being simply "drudges to the staff."[140] Four years later, an inspector said the half-day system was "very tiring for any but the grown up pupils."[141] In 1918 the same official said students were "worked too hard and taught too little."[142] In 1902 it was observed that while the students at Mount Elgin were working hard, they were not learning any skills.[143] At Coqualeetza, British Columbia, in 1906, the school matron complained that due to a lack of staff, the children were being taken out of class to do drudge work.[144]

The laundry room of the Brandon, Manitoba, school in 1946. *National Film Board of Canada, Photothèque, Library and Archives Canada, PA-048572.*

In Saskatchewan, Indian Commissioner W.A. Graham concluded that by 1916, the Qu'Appelle school had become little more than a workhouse. Over a forty-two-day period, the boys had attended class for only nine days, spending the rest of their time in the field.[145] Fourteen years later, he observed that at two Alberta schools, "The boys are being made slaves of, working too long hours and not receiving the close supervision they should have."[146]

The students were aware they were being worked, not trained. Of his days at the Kamloops school, George Manuel said, "Industrial training consisted of doing all the kinds of manual labour that are commonly done around a farm, except that we did not have the use of the equipment that even an Indian farmer of those days would have been using."[147] Clayton Mack attended the Alert Bay school in the 1920s. In addition to caring for the livestock, he "also helped look after the farm, helped with the potatoes, and helped cut the hay. I tried to go to school but there was not enough time. I worked most of the time. I went to Alert Bay for school and instead they put me in a job!"[148] Schools often competed for older students. When they could not get them, they put the younger students to

work. In 1945 Mount Elgin principal Reverend S.H. Soper pointed out that most of the students were under ten years of age. It was impossible, he wrote, "for these wee children to earn" what was needed to feed and clothe and warm themselves, and pay for repairs to farm equipment.[149]

The limited farm training the students received often was not appropriate for finding work when they returned home. For example, schools in British Columbia provided little training in fishing, even though many Aboriginal communities had active fisheries. Parents from northern Manitoba complained their children were not getting the training they would need to hunt and trap. As Martin Benson, an Indian Affairs education official, observed, the schools were actually making it harder for students to earn a living.[150] At some schools, it was not uncommon to keep female students on after they had graduated, until a suitable marriage had been arranged. During this period, they became full-time unpaid staff.[151]

The girls were worked hard as well. At the Lejac School, the girls spent most of the afternoons in the sewing room. In the 1927–1928 school year, they made 293 dresses, 191 aprons, 296 pairs of drawers, 301 chemises, and 600 pairs

In 1924 an Indian Agent in northern Manitoba said that a boy at the Mackay school in The Pas had been beaten "black from neck to his buttocks."
The General Synod Archives, Anglican Church of Canada, P7538-954.

of socks.[152] From the age of fourteen, Rita Joe spent much of her time working in the kitchen at the Shubenacadie school. "For that, you had to get up at four in the morning. We'd bake bread and—oh my God—every second day we'd bake about thirty-five or forty loaves. Holy Lord! And we made soup in a huge pot that was very high and very round. We'd make porridge in the morning, in a big, big porridge pot and we'd boil over two hundred eggs. It was a lot of hard work that we did in the kitchen and the cook could be cruel."[153] Domestic work could be dangerous. At Shubenacadie in 1930, two girls were taken to hospital when a dough mixer they were cleaning was started. In 1941 a girl at the same school was hospitalized when her hand was caught in a laundry wringer.[154]

For boys, the one advantage of fieldwork was that they were not supervised closely. They could speak their own language and be with their friends.[155] Arthur Ledoux recalled that during the planting and harvest seasons in Saskatchewan, "we were often obliged to spend the whole day at our work place, usually a welcome relief from the drudgery of classroom studies. Some of my fondest memories to this day are from the time spent working with my friends at the residence."[156]

Despite the fact that the half-day system was brought to an end in the 1950s, many schools retained their farm operations for several years. Its legacy was lasting: poorly housed and poorly nourished young students spent their time doing back-breaking, monotonous work to support schools that could not afford to educate them or train them. The experience of one former student, Solomon Johnston, speaks for thousands: "We cut wood, picked stones—all the worst jobs. We didn't learn anything. We didn't know anything. I read only a little now."[157]

Discipline: "He never should have gotten a licking like that."

In 1887 High River school principal Father Charles Claude reported that to impose order at the school, he had resorted to a system of military discipline, under which no breach of regulations went unpunished.[158] Those who violated the rules were subject to solitary confinement, the withholding of food, and, if necessary, beatings.[159] This regime was not out of step with an 1899 federal government directive that "corporal punishment

In 1934 the Shubenacadie principal had nineteen students flogged following a theft at the school. A judicial inquiry supported the principal's actions. *Nova Scotia Museum: Ethnology Collection.*

should only be resorted to in extreme cases. In ordinary cases the penalty might be solitary confinement for such time as the offence may warrant, or deprivation of certain articles of food allowed to other pupils."[160] A similar 1895 guideline had warned that corporal punishment should be administered only by the principal, should not include blows to the head, and should not result in bodily harm.[161] Over the system's history, several directives on discipline were issued. Despite this, the federal government showed limited interest in enforcing these guidelines. As a result, discipline in schools often exceeded the government's guidelines.

Corporal punishment was not uncommon in the nineteenth-century and even twentieth-century Canadian school system. In the 1880s, there were sixty strappings a month at Ottawa's Central School East. At the Jesse Ketchum public school in Toronto, "fighting, misbehaving in line, lying, eating in school, neglecting to correct wrong work, shooting peas in the classroom, going home when told to remain, long continued carelessness and general bad conduct" could fetch a student between four and twelve strokes on the palm of the hand.[162]

However, the residential schools bore a closer resemblance to schools for neglected, truant, or incorrigible children than to public schools. In the early twentieth century, boys who ran away from the Vancouver industrial school were flogged. Runaways from the Halifax school were strapped, and repeat offenders were placed in cells, and fed bread and water.[163] In the 1890s, there was a punishment room at the Mohawk Institute that measured six feet by ten feet, with one small light over the door.[164] In 1902 students at the Williams Lake residential school might be placed in a small room, and put on a bread-and-water diet for a few hours or up to twelve days.[165]

Even in an era when it commonly was held that to spare the rod was to spoil the child, many people considered the residential schools' discipline to be unnecessarily harsh. In 1896 an Indian agent said the behaviour of a teacher at the Red Deer school "would not be tolerated in a white school for a single day in any part of Canada." The agent was so alarmed by the teacher's behaviour that he kept a boy out of the school for fear he would be abused.[166] In 1914 a court in Brantford fined the principal of the Mohawk Institute $400 for confining two runaway girls in a cell for two days, and whipping one of them.[167]

These were not isolated events. A nurse found boys chained to benches for punishment at the Crowfoot school in 1921,[168] and at the Ahousaht school in the 1930s, an inspector reported that each member of the staff carried a strap.[169] At the Calgary school, all the students were put on bread and water in the early twentieth century when a laundress's moccasins disappeared (only to be found under a pile of magazines in her room a few days later).[170]

In 1934 a group of boys stole some money from a cash-box at the Shubenacadie school in Nova Scotia. Following a school investigation, nineteen boys were flogged with

> "
> *It was awful having to watch them holding back the tears and the hurt of not being able to help—or even talk to them.*
> "
>
> Isabelle Knockwood, former student

a seven-thonged strap made from harness leather. Most were then put on a bread-and-water diet for three days. A judicial inquiry, appointed in response to parental complaints, excused the principal's behaviour, even though, months later, many of the boys still bore bruises on their backs.[171]

Harsh discipline prompted children to run away, often at great risk to themselves. The coroner investigating the deaths of four boys who ran away from the Lejac school in British Columbia in 1937 called for an end to the school's "excessive corporal punishment."[172]

Runaways were subject to punishment and humiliation. In 1907 the principal of the Crowstand school in Saskatchewan caught a group of runaway boys, tied their hands together, and forced them to run behind his buggy back to the school.[173] Runaways from St. George's in British Columbia were chained together and forced to run back to school ahead of the principal. In other cases, runaways

were shackled to their beds.[174] In 1941 a boy who had run away from the Gordon's school in Saskatchewan, for fear of the principal, died of exposure.[175]

Upon their return, runaways often had their heads shaved. At the Shubenacadie school, girls checked at mealtimes to see if their brothers or cousins had been punished. According to Isabelle Knockwood, "You should have seen the look on the faces of the sisters and cousins of the boys who walked in that refectory with bald heads. It was awful having to watch them holding back the tears and the hurt of not being able to help—or even talk to them."[176] Raphael Ironstand recalled the shame of those whose heads had been shaved for speaking Cree in the 1950s. "Even though they wore scarves and toques to hide their heads, the tears were streaming down their faces. They were so embarrassed, they kept their heads bowed and eyes looking at the floor."[177]

Bedwetting was treated cruelly. In 1907 a boy who had been beaten for bedwetting ran away from the Norway House school. According to an Indian Affairs official, his feet were badly frozen, and it might have been necessary to amputate some toes.[178] Abraham Ruben had terrible nightmares on his first night at the Grollier Hall Residence in Inuvik. In the morning, he found he had wet his bed. When a nun discovered what he had done, Ruben said she slapped him in the face, and called him "a dirty pig."[179] Mabel James's saddest memory of St. Michael's school "was to watch my cousin Mary and others get a spanking because of wetting the bed. They stood in line for a spanking with a hairbrush. They held their bundle of wet sheets under their arm."[180] These punishments continued through the system's history. One boy recalled that when he came to the Kamloops school in 1969, "I started wetting the bed. What was really bad about it was I couldn't stop. I wanted to. I tried everything. They would take our sheets and wrap them around our heads and make us walk past all the other kids."[181]

There are also many accounts of teachers striking students with rulers and pointers in the classroom. One Métis student from Alberta was daydreaming when "I was brought to my senses with a yardstick smashed across my back, just right about where my shoulders are."[182] At St. Philip's School in Fort George, Quebec, a frail-looking teacher was adept at rousing inattentive students with a quick rap on the knuckles with her ruler.[183] At Kamloops, Janie Marchand recalled how a beloved teacher was replaced with one who "was mean, you couldn't do anything, she'd whack you. Oh, she always had a little stick."[184]

Simon Baker and his friends ran away from the Lytton, British Columbia, school after witnessing a friend being beaten with a leather strap. According to Baker, "Maybe he did a naughty thing, but he never should have gotten a licking like that." *Department of Mines and Technical Surveys, Library and Archives Canada, PA-020080.*

Ear pulling was another common form of discipline; according to a former Shubenacadie student, "Jesus! I used to hate them earpulls—your ear would feel like it was going to pop off—it would hurt right in the centre core. They used to like to pull ears and twist."[185] In 1912 at Round Lake school, the principal's wife, who was working as the matron, struck a girl so hard in the ear she was knocked to the floor. A church investigation concluded that neither the principal nor his wife could control their tempers.[186]

For much of the period the schools operated, the federal government did not provide clear direction on discipline. By the 1930s, when a principal wrote to Indian Affairs looking for such direction, the department was forced to admit that while it had issued a circular on discipline several years earlier, it could not find a current copy of it.[187] On occasion, Indian Affairs officials thought their superiors were not prepared to take on the churches when principals were found to be using too much force. In 1919, when a boy who ran away from the Anglican Old Sun school was shackled to his bed and beaten with a horsewhip until his back bled, Indian Commissioner W.A. Graham tried, without success, to have the principal fired.[188] In 1924 no action was taken when the Indian

agent reported that a boy at the Anglican school in The Pas had been beaten "black from neck to his buttocks."[189] The lack of support from Ottawa led Graham to complain that there was no point in reporting abuses since the department was too willing to accept whatever excuses the principals offered up.[190]

In the 1940s, discipline at the Brandon school was a constant source of complaint. On one occasion, four girls froze their feet in an attempt to escape the school. Parents in Saskatchewan, alarmed by reports of harsh discipline at the school, stopped sending their children there in protest. When the department sent out an inspector to discover why children kept on running away from the school, the principal prevented him from speaking to staff members in private, and allowed him to speak only to handpicked students. An Indian Affairs inspector eventually concluded that the principal was an aggressive, aloof disciplinarian. Even as the complaints continued to pile up, the principal, who had been the subject of complaints when he was principal of the Mount Elgin school, remained in office until 1955—when the church simply transferred him to a new school.[191]

Such policy as existed was usually reactive. In 1947 a serious beating given to a student at the Morley school

In the 1940s parents in Saskatchewan refused to send their children to the Brandon school because they felt their children were being mistreated at the school. *National Film Board of Canada, Photothèque, Library and Archives Canada, PA-048560.*

in Alberta led Indian Affairs to issue a policy directive on corporal punishment, which set out the type of strap that could be used, the number of blows that could be administered (no more than four per hand for students over fourteen), who could strap students, and a requirement that punishment be recorded.[192]

This new policy did not prevent continued abuses. In 1953 two boys who ran away from the Birtle school were beaten badly. The Indian Affairs inspector of schools thought the principal had overstepped his bounds, but his behaviour was excused on the grounds that he had to make an example of the boys, since they had been caught running away.[193] A decade later, the principal at Cecilia Jeffrey school in northwestern Ontario was locking runaways in a room with only a mattress, taking away all their clothing (save their underwear), and putting them on a bread-and-milk diet. Students such as Pearl Achneepineskum have strong memories of corporal punishment at Cecilia Jeffrey during this period: "I knew the strap, because a man strapped me with the same one across my bare buttocks ten times because I made a noise after the lights were out."[194]

Abuse: "I felt so dirty."

In October 1990, Phil Fontaine, the Grand Chief of the Assembly of Manitoba Chiefs, called for a national inquiry into the residential school system. His call garnered national attention, particularly because he spoke of the sexual abuse he had experienced as a student at the Fort Alexander school in Manitoba. When asked how extensive that abuse had been, he replied, "If we took an example, my Grade 3 class, if there were twenty boys in this particular class, every single one of the twenty would have experienced what I experienced." Chief Fontaine also spoke of the physical abuse many students had undergone, and the way the schools deprived children of their culture. Most tellingly, he spoke of how that abuse had had lasting impacts on his life and the lives of all other former students. His coming forward, he hoped, would make it easier for others to talk about their experiences.[195]

Aboriginal people had been raising concerns about residential schools since the Canadian government and the leading Christian churches of the day established the schools in the nineteenth century. However, until Chief Fontaine spoke out, that criticism largely had been ignored. His statement also gave support to an Aboriginal movement for justice that had been building since the 1980s. In 1994 the Assembly of First Nations released

In 1990 Phil Fontaine, the Grand Chief of the Assembly of Manitoba Chiefs, drew national attention to the residential school issue by speaking of the abuse he and his fellow students had undergone at the Fort Alexander, Manitoba, school. *Provincial Archives of Manitoba, N14950.*

Breaking the Silence: An Interpretive Study of Residential School Impact and Healing as Illustrated by the Stories of First Nation Individuals. Starting in the mid-1990s, former students began making legal claims for compensation for abuse experienced while they were at the schools. By 2002 over 12,000 former students had filed claims.[196]

Until recently, public discussion of the sexual abuse of children, particularly of vulnerable children in institutions such as orphanages, residential schools, or jails, has been rare. The official records of the residential school system make little reference to incidents of such abuse. The victims often had no one to turn to, and the perpetrators were the very people who held authority over every aspect of their lives. In many cases, their parents either feared or respected the church officials who ran the schools. For example, after his first year at Grollier Hall in Inuvik, Abraham Ruben told his mother about the abuse and beatings there. Outraged, she took her concerns to the local priest, who reassured her the children were being well taken care of at the school.[197]

Evidence of the problem was there from the beginning. In 1868 charges of sexually violating two students were laid against the principal of the Anglican orphanage at Great Bear Lake in Rupert's Land, leading to the orphanage's closure.[198] In 1884 the Oblates hired Jean L'Heureux to recruit the first students to attend the High River school,

despite the fact they had forced him earlier to leave one of their missions due to sexual misbehaviour. An Anglican pastor accused L'Heureux of "practicing immorality of a most beastly type" while he was the school recruiter.[199]

In 1899 the principal of the Rupert's Land school was dismissed following complaints from members of the St. Peter's Band in Manitoba that he was kissing the girls (as well as beating other students).[200] Fifteen years later, Oblate official Henri Grandin accused High River principal George Nordmann of neglecting his duties "in order to play with little girls in your room, or to read magazines."[201]

Although the Crowstand school principal fired the farm instructor in 1914 for having sexual intercourse with female students in his room and the dormitory, there were other cases where abuse was tolerated.[202] At the Cecilia Jeffrey school in northwestern Ontario, in 1922, students complained to the assistant matron that the principal had "put their hands under his clothing" and was in the habit of kissing them.[203] Following complaints from the local First Nation, Indian Affairs concluded the principal should be replaced. The Presbyterian Church argued that to dismiss him at that point would be seen by the band as a "direct result of their appeal to the Department." To allow the church to save face, the principal continued in the job for another six months.[204]

The principal of the Rupert's Land school in Manitoba was fired in 1899 after he was accused of kissing female students. *Provincial Archives of Manitoba, N16969.*

It was difficult for students to have their concerns taken seriously. When Rita Arey complained that a well-liked priest in the Northwest Territories had been grabbing her and rubbing up against her when he passed by, she was told "it was just his way."[205] When a female student who had been sexually assaulted by a staff member at the Kamloops school reported the matter to a supervisor, she met with a priest who, she recounts, told her to keep quiet about the assault. When the abuse resumed several months later, she and a number of girls banded together. "We made a plan that all ten of us would stick together and not leave each other anymore. If we hung out together no one would bother us, so that's what we did, because none of us were allowed to speak."[206] At Fort Alexander in the 1950s, younger boys were sent to one of the priests for what was termed "ménage," during which he would wash their genitals. Ted Fontaine recalled that the practice did not end until "we became older and bigger, and our determination to threaten, maim, hurt or even kill our tormentors gave us the power to refuse the treatment."[207]

Not all students report such abuse. Ben Stonechild attended the File Hills school in Saskatchewan until its closure in 1949. According to him, "We weren't molested in any way at the schools. It wasn't like the stories you hear at other places."[208]

The church and government preferred to deal with these matters as quietly as possible. When they took action, dismissal—or, in some cases, transfers—rather than prosecution of individuals was the norm. The lack of publicity often made it possible for a dismissed abuser to find work at another school in another part of the country. If the abuser held a position of authority in the school, he or she might preside over a reign of terror. For example, as the director of the Gordon residential school from 1968 to 1984, William Penniston Starr instituted a system of rewards and punishments as part of his systematic sexual abuse of boys between the ages of seven and fourteen. In 1993 he was convicted on ten counts of abuse.[209]

Although there had been the occasional prosecution in the past, it was not until the late 1980s that the courts caught up with many predators. In 1988 Derek

In 1998 three Grollier Hall staff members in Inuvik, Northwest Territories, were convicted of sexually abusing students. *Northwest Territories Archives, Jerome, N-1987-017: 2241.*

Clarke, a former employee of the Lytton residential school in British Columbia, pleaded guilty to sexual abuse charges. In 1995 the Royal Canadian Mounted Police initiated an investigation into all residential schools in British Columbia. By 2003, it had investigated over 900 abuse claims. Fourteen charges were laid, and jail sentences were imposed on eight former staff.[210] The staff had worked at the Roman Catholic schools at Williams Lake, Kuper Island, and Lower Post; the Anglican school at Lytton; and the United Church school at Port Alberni. In addition, former staff at the Roman Catholic Grollier Hall in Inuvik in the Northwest Territories, the Anglican school at Pelican Lake, the Roman Catholic school at St. Anne in Ontario, and the Roman Catholic Coudert Hall in Whitehorse, Yukon, also have been convicted on indecent assault charges.[211] In many other instances, cases did not proceed because the alleged perpetrators had died or because, with the passage of time, government lawyers concluded there was insufficient evidence on which to base a prosecution.

Overall, the residential school system often amounted to a system of institutionalized child neglect, compounded by the behaviour of specific individuals who used their authority and the isolation of the schools to physically and sexually abuse those in their care. Within this context, students could be prey not only to abuse from staff, but also from older or better organized students. Abuse of students by other students could range from bullying and beating to sexual abuse. The extent of such abuse in the residential school system has yet to be explored.

In some schools, a culture of abuse permeated the entire institution. Within a week of his arrival at residential school, seven-year-old Greg Murdock from Fisher River, Manitoba, was raped by a group of older boys. When he reported the assault to the school staff, the boys beat him, and subjected him to another assault. Concluding that the school could not protect him, he simply stopped reporting further abuse.[212] Where a climate of abuse existed, bullying was another common problem. Simon Baker, who went to the Lytton school in British Columbia, wrote: "When I was young, I sometimes got beat up by the older boys for something they said I did wrong."[213] Shirley Bear remembered the All Saints school in Prince Albert as an unhappy place. "I was shocked by all the fighting and bullying that went on. I learned to keep my mouth shut when I knew who did things they were not supposed to do."[214] One seven-year-old student at Williams Lake was beaten and assaulted by other students in a toilet stall. "I remember feeling the ugliness. I guess at that time I didn't understand what it was, but it hurt and I felt so dirty." Upon telling the principal what happened, the student was told to ask for forgiveness.[215] At the Grouard school in Alberta, it seemed to one student that everyone always was fighting. "You were always caged around by a big ten-foot-high fence. You're sort of caged animals, I guess."[216]

Following the conviction of a former dormitory supervisor at the Port Alberni, British Columbia, school, former students successfully sued both the Canadian government and the United Church. *The United Church of Canada Archives, 93.049P510. (1941).*

In many schools, food was used to buy friendship or protection. Phil Fontaine recalled, "Some kids never got to eat any lard because they had to be protected during their entire time in school. Fruit was the same, you could buy protection with an apple."[217] At the Kamloops school, Andrew Amos "learned to cope with the resident bullies who always picked on us and took our extras, such as apples, oranges, even slices of bread."[218]

The sexual and physical abuse of students by staff and other students represents the most extreme failings of the residential school system. In an underfunded, under-supervised system, there was little to protect children from predators. The victims often were treated as liars or troublemakers. Students were taught to be quiet to protect themselves.

The impacts were devastating, and continue to be felt today. Long after abuse stops, people who were abused as children remain prey to feelings of shame and fear, increased susceptibility to a range of diseases, and emotional distress. Those who have been abused run a greater risk of abusing, and have difficulty forming healthy emotional attachments.[219]

Accomplishment: "My experience at the residential school was good."

Although the residential school system was a destructive system, the schools were not absolutely destructive. Between 2009 and 2011, many students have come forward to express their gratitude to former teachers at the Truth and Reconciliation Commission events. Their testimony is a reminder that not all residential school experiences are identical. Although few students went to residential school willingly, once they were there, there were activities—sports, arts, reading, dancing, writing—that many students came to enjoy. Even after they were old enough to leave, some chose to stay in school and complete their education. In certain cases, students developed lifelong relationships with their former teachers. Others not only finished high school, they pursued post-secondary education. Some went on to take leadership positions in Aboriginal organizations, the churches, and in society at large. Despite the shortcomings of the system, some students were able to adjust to it, and others achieved significant accomplishments. These positive experiences stand in the shadow of

The Battleford, Saskatchewan, school cricket team in 1895. In 1899, an Indian Affairs official wrote of the Battleford school, "A noticeable feature of this school is its games. They are all thoroughly and distinctly 'white'. The boys use the boxing gloves with no little science, and excellent temper and play good games of cricket and football with great interest and truly Anglo-Saxon vigor." *Canada, Ernest Maunder, David Ewens collection, Library and Archives Canada, PA-182265.*

the system's overall failings, but they are also part of the residential school story.

Children who faced difficult home situations sometimes have more positive assessments of residential schools. In 1944 twelve-year-old Rita Joe, an orphan, was living with relatives who alternately abused and neglected her. Fearful, she called the Indian agent and asked if he could arrange to have her admitted to the Shubenacadie school in Nova Scotia.[220] Joe acknowledged that many negative things happened at the school, but she never regretted going there.[221] In 1956, as a young mother with four children under six years of age, she and her husband Frank decided to send their oldest daughter to Shubenacadie. "We knew she would get an education there, and would be cared for until we were better off."[222]

Like Rita and Frank Joe, many other parents used residential schools as part of a family survival strategy. Louis Calihoo, a Métis man who went north to the Klondike in 1898 to make money during the Gold Rush, placed his sons in the Grouard school.[223] During the Great Depression of the 1930s, a Chilcotin father wrote his son in residential school, "I didn't make much money this year, just enough to buy grub to live on. You are lucky to be in school where

you get plenty to eat. If you were home you would get hungry many days."[224]

Florence Bird was born to Métis parents in Fort Chipewyan in 1899. After the death of her father Joseph in 1909, she was raised in the Holy Angels Convent at Fort Chipewyan. A sickly child, she thought she would not have survived without the convent. "There were lots of pitiful kids in those days. The orphans were more pitiful than everybody else because they were badly treated by the people and even by the relatives sometimes." Although the nuns were strict, she thought that with so many children to supervise, they had few options.[225] Martha Mercredi was another orphaned Métis child who was raised in Holy Angels. "I was never lonely because I took to the nuns as my own relatives. Sister Superior was my grandmother and Sister Lucy was the teacher and she was like my momma, she's the one that's my guardian. So I have no complaint about the convent. I am very glad that they showed me how to read and write."[226]

Students involved in sports, music, drama, and dance found that these activities helped them maintain a sense of their own value, and were sources of strength in later life.[227] Andrew Amos recalled that at the Kamloops

A student at the All Saints School in Aklavik, Northwest Territories, taking his Cub Scout oath. *The General Synod Archives, Anglican Church of Canada, P7538-832.*

The Old Sun school School softball team in the 1940s. *The General Synod Archives, Anglican Church of Canada, P75-103 (S7-202).*

school, "The treatment was good as long as you excelled in sports." He went on to become a provincial boxing champion. Travelling to fights and games allowed students to leave the school and see other parts of the province. Amos recalled, "It was through competitive sports, and the girls with their dancing and travel, that we were able to cope and survive the daily routine of life at the residential school."[228] Even if they were poorly equipped, residential school hockey, football, and baseball teams provided many students with a refuge and a source of pride. Alex, a student at the St.-Marc-de-Figuery school in Amos, Quebec, said, "At the residential school, if it wasn't for hockey, I would have gone crazy. Sport became my support. Until I was thirty years old, I played and when I was on the ice, I would let it all out."[229] The prejudices of the day meant that girls enjoyed fewer athletic opportunities. The Kamloops school was known for its dance program. Vivian Ignace, one of the dancers, had mixed feelings about her experience, noting that dancers were not allowed to participate in sports for fear of injury. Despite this, she concluded that "through that experience with the Kamloops Indian Residential School Dancers, I learned some assertiveness skills. I learned to smile even

when I wasn't happy. I learned to get along and talk with people and that was good. I learned a lot through that Irish nun."[230]

Some students were grateful for the religious instruction they received. Edna Gregoire, who attended the Kamloops school, for example, said, "My experience at the residential school was good. That's one thing I'll tell you, it was really good to be able to go to school and to learn how to read and write. And the other thing, the best of all, I was happy to learn about God."[231] Margaret Stonechild recalled the File Hills, Saskatchewan, principal as a very good religious instructor. "I am eternally grateful for that because I have a firm standing in Christian beliefs to this day."[232] Bernard Pinay said that at File Hills, he never felt religion was being forced down his throat.[233] Some parents, at the urging of missionaries, sent their children to residential school specifically for a religious education.[234]

In some cases, strong personal relationships developed between students and staff. Eleanor Brass's parents, Fred and Marybelle Dieter, were married at the File Hills boarding school where Kate Gillespie, the principal, and her sister Janet (the school matron) made the wedding arrangements, and baked the wedding cake.[235] Shirley Bear recalled one principal of the Prince Albert school as a tyrant. However, "The next principal, Rev. A.J. Serase, was an angel. After he came, the whole system changed. He was just like a father to the students. He was the minister who married my husband and me."[236]

Many students, either on their own or with the encouragement of a well-remembered teacher, developed a love of learning. Jane Willis, at the Anglican school at Fort George on James Bay, credits her decision to complete

The girls' marching band at the Cardston, Alberta, school, 1952. *The General Synod Archives, Anglican Church of Canada, P2004-09 (143).*

her education to one of her teachers, who worked hard to develop students' self-confidence. "Learning was a pleasure with Mr. Woods as our cheerleader and coach. He urged us to ask questions, to take an active part in class instead of sitting back and taking his word for everything."[237] At the Moose Factory School in Ontario, Billy Diamond became a voracious reader. When the time came for him to move on to high school in Sault Ste. Marie, he saw it as an opportunity for adventure, learning, and meeting new friends. Once there, he helped form an Indian student council. Diamond went on, as leader of the James Bay Cree, to negotiate the 1975 James Bay and Northern Quebec Agreement, Canada's first comprehensive land-claims agreement.[238] While the residential school experience left him feeling embarrassed about his culture, Peter Irniq described the education he received in Chesterfield Inlet as "top-notch." "As much as that particular teacher used to call us bloody dodos and no good for nothing, a bunch of hounds of iniquity, he taught us pretty good in terms of English."[239]

The system's overall educational success was limited, but throughout its history, numerous determined individuals pursued their education beyond residential school. Daniel Kennedy, who described his introduction into residential schooling as being "lassoed, roped and taken to the Government School at Lebret," went on to study at Saint Boniface College. By 1899 he was an

interpreter for Indian Affairs. In 1906 he helped local First Nations overcome the opposition of local Indian Affairs officials and successfully petition the federal government to be allowed to hold feasts and sports days.[240]

Kennedy did not enter the priesthood, but other residential school students did pursue religious careers. Edward Ahenakew, who attended Emmanuel College in Prince Albert, was ordained as an Anglican minister in 1910.[241] Peter Kelly, a graduate of the Coqualeetza Institute in Sardis, British Columbia, became a United Church minister, eventually serving as president of the British Columbia Conference of the United Church of Canada. He also played an important role in presenting First Nations land concerns to the federal government in 1911 and 1927. Kelly was not uncritical of the church's Aboriginal work, noting in 1958 that in too many cases, the church was sending misfits, who did not make the grade elsewhere, to work as ministers and teachers in Aboriginal communities.[242] Stan McKay, who attended the Brandon school, became the first Aboriginal moderator of the United Church of Canada in 1992.

Ahab Spence's career bridged religion, government service, and First Nations politics. After attending Anglican schools at Elkhorn and The Pas, Manitoba, he became an Anglican archdeacon, an employee of both the Saskatchewan and federal governments, and, in 1974, the president of the Manitoba Indian Brotherhood.[243]

The student cast of the play *Isle of Jewels* at the Coqualeetza, British Columbia, school. *The United Church of Canada Archives, 93.049P424N. (19--?)*

Many other Aboriginal leaders attended residential schools, and while they may have developed leadership skills in the schools, they often also became the system's harshest critics.

The Roman Catholic Grandin College in Fort Smith, Northwest Territories, had one of the best reputations of any school. Established in 1960 as a preparatory school for Aboriginal priests and nuns, Grandin College's first director decided to turn it into a leadership training centre. The use of Aboriginal languages was common throughout the school, and students were encouraged to excel. Ethel Blondin-Andrew, the first Aboriginal woman to serve as a federal cabinet minister, said she was "saved" by Grandin College, where she "learned that discipline, including physical fitness, was essential."[244] She was just one of a number of Grandin graduates who went on to play leading roles in public life in the North. Others include former Northwest Territories premiers, ministers, Dene Nation presidents, and official language commissioners.[245]

The individual student's ability to succeed within the residential school system, and the positive difference that individual teachers and school staff made in some students' lives, are important parts of the history and legacy of the schools and deserve recognition.

Resistance: "I don't ever want to see cruelty like this again."

It was at Aboriginal insistence that provisions for schools were included in the treaties. They wanted on-reserve schools that would give young people the skills to help their people in their dealings with settler society. They never envisioned a school system that separated children from their parents, their language, and their cultural and spiritual practices. In some cases, they bluntly told Indian Affairs officials they did not want their children to become like white people.[246] Not surprisingly, many Aboriginal parents opposed residential schooling from the outset.

First, they simply refused to send their children to residential school. An 1897 Indian Affairs official's report said a Saulteaux-Cree chief "will not allow his children to be sent to school, says he would sooner see them dead, and on every chance he gets speaks against education and the Industrial Schools provided by the Government."[247] For much of the system's early years, principals spent much of their time and energy recruiting students. Father Albert Lacombe, the founding principal of the High River school in Alberta, lamented his difficulties in recruiting students.[248] The principal of the Shingwauk school complained in 1888 that it should not be necessary for him "to be going around seeking, and in many cases, begging, and often begging in vain, for pupils from indifferent, and often opposing parents."[249] Over sixty years later, in the fall of 1948, the principal of the school in Prince Albert, Saskatchewan, travelled over 1600 miles, recruiting students.[250]

Often the only way principals could recruit children was to pay parents. In the 1880s, Father Lacombe offered gifts and presents.[251] In 1906 Brandon school principal Thompson Ferrier was giving parents gifts if they sent

> **"**
>
> *He sent me to hide in the woods. He told the Indian agent I wasn't home which was true. I was hiding in a hollow stump. I waited until the plane left.*
>
> **"**
>
> Mabel James, former student

their children to the school.[252] Fred Dieter's parents took money from the principals of both the File Hills and Qu'Appelle schools in Saskatchewan, before deciding to send their son to the closest school.[253]

Parents and grandparents often withdrew children from school if they thought they were not being well treated. When, in the 1870s, Charles Nowell ran away from the Alert Bay, British Columbia, school after being beaten and locked up for swearing at the principal's wife, the principal followed him to his grandfather's home. There, his grandfather, alerted by Charles that he was facing another beating, grabbed a piece of wood and chased the principal away. Charles returned to school only after his grandfather extracted a promise from the principal that the boy could be physically punished only if he had been very disobedient.[254] Angela Sidney's father took her out of the Choutla school in the Yukon in its early years. "That

was because my sister died there, so my father blamed the school because they didn't get help soon enough."[255] When a child from the Old Crow community died at Choutla in the 1920s, the community stopped sending children to the school for twenty-five years.[256]

In 1922 the Mounted Police and the local Indian agent were drawn into a conflict between anxious Haisla parents and the administrators of the Elizabeth Long Home in Kitimaat, British Columba. The death of a young girl had prompted the parents, already concerned by previous deaths and illnesses at the school, to pull their children from the school. The walkout ended only when the parents succeeded in getting a written assurance from the matron that "the children got all the food they wanted, that they would be well cared for, and be supplied with sufficient clothing."[257]

In 1959, eighty years after Charles Nowell's grandfather protected him from the Alert Bay principal, Mabel James's grandfather rescued her from the same school. When the plane came to her community to collect students to return to school at the end of summer, she told her grandfather she hated the school. "He sent me to hide in the woods. He told the Indian agent I wasn't home which was true. I was hiding in a hollow stump. I waited until the plane left."[258]

Sometimes parents fought back. When visiting his daughter at the File Hills school in Saskatchewan in the early twentieth century, Fred Dieter noticed that a girl's legs had been shackled together to prevent her running away. He bounded up the stairs to the principal's office, grabbed him, and ordered him to "Take those chains off that child." He left with the warning that the principal was lucky to get off with a good shaking. "These are children, not criminals, and I don't ever want to see cruelty like this again."[259]

Parents also resisted by campaigning for the establishment of a local day school. In 1921 all the school-aged children in the Whitefish River Reserve in Ontario were sent to residential school. The following year, the band petitioned to have a day school on the reserve. After being initially turned down, the request was granted in 1924.[260] When the Delmas, Saskatchewan, school burned down in 1948, there was local controversy as to whether it should be rebuilt or replaced with day schools. John Tootoosis collected names on a pro-day-school petition, and the local priest, who had already threatened to excommunicate him for his criticism of residential schools, accused Tootoosis of doing the devil's work.[261]

Pupils and staff of the Elizabeth Long Memorial House in Kitimaat, British Columbia, in 1922. In that year, parents pulled their children out of the school following the death of a student. *The United Church of Canada Archives, 93.049P458.*

Parents also wrote letters of complaint to Ottawa about food and health in residential schools, starting as early as 1889.[262] In voicing these complaints, parents had to overcome their worries that by speaking out, they would be making matters worse for their children.[263]

When Aboriginal people began to organize politically, criticism of residential schooling always emerged as a key issue. In Brantford, the Six Nations formed the Indian's Rights Association, which hired inspectors to ensure the public school curriculum was taught in the Mohawk Institute in the early twentieth century.[264] In 1909 F.O. Loft, a former residential school student and future founder of the League of Indians of Canada, wrote a series of articles in *Saturday Night* magazine, in which he described the residential schools as death traps, and recommended their replacement with day schools.[265] At its 1931 meeting, the League of Indians of Western Canada passed a resolution calling for the creation of more day schools to replace the residential schools. The following year, delegates called for improvements in the qualifications of residential school teachers.[266]

Parents also sought legal help in their conflicts with the schools. In 1921 the Grand General Indian Council of Ontario hired a lawyer to act on behalf of parents who claimed that children at the Chapleau school were being punished cruelly and worked too hard.[267] A former Shubenacadie student used a lawyer to lobby, successfully, to prevent his siblings from being sent to the school in 1936.[268] Parents of students at the Birtle school hired a lawyer in 1938 because they believed their children were not learning practical skills at school.[269] In 1943 parents of children at Mount Elgin brought their concerns over the behaviour of the school principal before the local justice of the peace.[270]

Students expressed their resistance in a variety of ways. Some, like Billy Diamond at the school at Moose Factory, Ontario, protested the change from a traditional to Euro-Canadian diet by not eating.[271] Others supplemented their diets with kitchen raids. At the Lytton school in British Columbia, Simon Baker convinced a group of hungry and overworked boys that the only way they could improve their rations was to threaten a strike. Baker told the principal that since they were being worked like men, they should be fed like men. If the students did not get an improvement in diet, Baker warned, they would steal the food. The principal complimented Baker on his honesty, and agreed to their demands.[272]

In some cases, students lobbied for changes. When supervisors at the Edmonton Methodist school refused to listen to student demands for change in the school

Parents brought their complaints about the principal of the Mount Elgin, Ontario, school before a justice of the peace in 1943. *The United Church of Canada Archives, 90.162P1167N. (n.d.)*

routine, the students rebelled. According to Rosa Bell, "They broke into the kitchen and threw pork everywhere. They also destroyed the supervisor's supply of food, which was different from the food given to us. Some older boys brought us ice cream during the raid. We had never tasted ice cream! The rebellion was successful and a meeting was held to discuss the changes."[273]

From the very beginning of the residential school system, children ran away. During the 1885 Northwest Rebellion, all the students left the Battleford and High River schools. In 1900 Tom Longboat, perhaps Canada's most well-known runner, ran away from the Mohawk Institute twice. After the second time, he never returned.[274] Sometimes, students engaged in mass escapes: in 1953 thirty-two boys ran away from a Saskatchewan school; a decade later, a dozen ran away from a school in north-western Ontario.[275]

Runaways often took tremendous risks. In 1902 nine boys ran away from the Williams Lake, BC, school. Eight were captured, but the ninth, Duncan Sticks, an eight-year-old boy from Alkali Lake, froze to death.[276] In 1941 John Kicki, Michael Sutherland, and Michael Matinas ran away from the Fort Albany school; they were never found.[277] Two girls drowned trying to get away from the Kuper Island school.[278] In 1966 twelve-year-old Charlie

Wenjack died trying to make his way back to his home community from the Cecilia Jeffrey school in Kenora.[279] Joseph Commanda died when he was hit by a train in Toronto after running away from the Mohawk Institute in 1968.[280] In 1970 two more boys who ran away from the Cecilia Jeffrey school died.[281]

Almost every child dreamed of going home. Some, such as Raphael Ironstand at the Pine Creek school in Manitoba, stayed only because they were too far from home.[282] Others thought about running away, but were too frightened by the punishments given to runaways. Donna Roberts, a Métis student at the St. Henri school in Alberta, said all the students were required to witness the punishment that was given to two runaway boys. "After that, people didn't run away because they knew what they were going to get."[283] Geraldine Sanderson, who attended the Gordon's school in Saskatchewan in the 1960s, recalled that she and some other students "took a pony from a farmer's yard and rode it for several nights trying to get home. We hardly ever made it home, we were usually caught." Once caught, the students' heads were shaved. "It was awful. I felt very ashamed. We also had to scrub the stairs with a toothbrush."[284]

One of the most dramatic forms of resistance was to burn the school down. There were over fifty major fires

Charlie Nowell ran away from the Alert Bay school in the 1870s after he was beaten by the principal. This photo was taken at the school in 1885.
George M. Dawson, Geological Survey of Canada collection, Library and Archives Canada, PA-037934.

at residential schools. Students were responsible for fires at Saint-Paul-des-Métis, Alert Bay, Kuper Island (students burned the school down when holidays were cancelled), the Mohawk Institute, Mount Elgin, Delmas, and Lac la Ronge. In commenting on the safety of the St. Alban's school in Prince Albert, an inspector wrote, "More than one disastrous Indian school fire has been started by the pupils themselves in an effort to obtain their freedom from a school which they did not like." Given the large number of students who were running away from the school, he worried that a dissatisfied student might try to set the school on fire.[285]

Some students fought back. In 1902 a federal government inspector said that at the Red Deer, Alberta, school, the older students swore, disrupted prayers, and threatened teachers. The situation was so out of control that one teacher successfully prosecuted a student for assault.[286] Near the end of her stay in a Roman Catholic residence in the Northwest Territories, Alice Blondin-Perrin found herself in a conflict with a nun, who was demanding that she and a fellow student get down on their knees and beg God for forgiveness. As the confrontation heightened, she grabbed a broom and swung it at the nun, narrowly missing her. From that point on, she felt that the girls were treated more fairly. "That year I learned to stand up for myself and the other girls."[287]

Resistance was continuous throughout the life of the system. Parents lobbied for day schools, for on-reserve boarding schools, for better food, less discipline, more education, and less drudgery. Students looked for ways to frustrate their teachers, get more to eat, ease their workloads, and get back to their families. Much of their resistance was passive, ranging from dawdling when returning from chores to refusals to do assignments. But it could also be aggressive, as students and parents physically confronted staff, and even, at times, destructive and dangerous, such as those occasions when students burned down the school. Resistance may have led to improvements in the system, but never overturned the balance of power. This resistance—the refusal to be assimilated—was shown in the community, in the classroom, in the playground, in the kitchen, and in the fields. It was a central force in driving federal officials finally to recognize that residential schooling had been an irredeemable failure.

CHAPTER THREE

Residential Schools in the North and the Arctic

The Sacred Heart School at Fort Providence in the Northwest Territories was established in 1867. This photograph shows children playing at the school in the 1920s. *F.H. Kitto, Canada. Department of Indian and Northern Affairs, Library and Archives Canada, PA-101548.*

In Canada, the North has been an ever-shifting concept. In 1876 the North-West Territories included all of present-day Alberta, Saskatchewan, and the Yukon and Northwest Territories, as well as most of present-day Manitoba, Ontario, and Quebec, and Nunavut. As settlement increased, new provinces were created out of the territories, portions of the territories were added to existing provinces, and the territories were subdivided. Today, northern Canada is made up of three territories—Yukon (created in 1898), the Northwest Territories (the name was changed from the North-West Territories in 1912), and Nunavut (created in 1999)—and portions of Quebec and Newfoundland and Labrador that extend into the Ungava peninsula. The Quebec portion of the Canadian North is known as Nunavik, while the Newfoundland and Labrador portion is known as Nunatsiavut. Residential schools operated throughout the North.

The Canadian government's policy of assimilating Aboriginal peoples was not applied in a uniform manner. In the North, as long as there was no demand for Aboriginal land, the federal policy was to delay taking on the financial obligations that came with treaties. The expectation was that Aboriginal people would continue to trap, trade, and live off the land.[1] In 1909 Indian Affairs minister Frank Oliver said, in response to a request to establish a residential school in the Yukon, "I will not undertake in a general way to educate the Indians of the Yukon. In my judgement they can, if left as Indians, earn a better living."[2]

The residential schooling experience in the North can be divided into two periods: the missionary period, which ended in the mid-1950s; and the modern period, which was initiated by the federal government in the 1950s.

The Choutla school at Carcross in the Yukon was the first government-funded Anglican residential school in the North. *The General Synod Archives, Anglican Church of Canada, 7538 (892).*

The Missionary Period

During the missionary period, residential schooling was limited to the Yukon and the Mackenzie Valley in the Northwest Territories, the shore of James Bay in Quebec, and Labrador. No residential schools were established in the eastern regions of present-day Nunavut during this period, which ended in the 1950s. The Sacred Heart School at Fort Providence (on the Mackenzie River, near Great Slave Lake) was the first residential school in what is now the Northwest Territories (NWT). The school, which took in its first students in 1867—the same year as Canadian Confederation—was founded by Oblate missionaries, but its daily operations depended on the work of Grey Nuns, who served as teachers and nurses. Originally intended for the children of Hudson's Bay Company (HBC) managers and their employees, most of whom were Métis, it also served as a home for orphaned Dene children. By 1889 the number of orphaned Aboriginal students at the school at Providence exceeded the children of the HBC employees.[3]

Life was not easy at Sacred Heart. During the school's second year, there was no meat, no flour, no potatoes, no butter, and no grease, causing many Métis parents to worry about the treatment their children were receiving. In 1881, were it not for a 15,000-franc donation from the Catholic Society for the Propagation of the Faith in France, the cash-strapped Oblates would have had to close the school.[4] The school's financial situation was eased somewhat in 1896 when the federal government began to provide funding.[5]

Education was central to the ongoing contest between the Anglican and Roman Catholic missionaries for Aboriginal converts in the Northwest Territories. While the Roman Catholics established their dominance in the Mackenzie Valley, the Anglicans enjoyed more success in the eastern and central Arctic, and the Yukon Territory. There were no Methodist, Presbyterian, or United Church residential schools in the North.

The first successful Anglican school in the North started in a modest way at the Forty Mile Mission in the Yukon, when Bishop William Carpenter Bompas began boarding Aboriginal children in his home in 1891.[6] By 1894 there were six students, four of whom were Métis.[7] In 1903 Bompas transferred the students to his new mission in Carcross. There, he commenced a decade-long campaign for the establishment of a government-funded residential school that led, in 1911, to the opening of the Choutla school.[8]

Students at the Shingle Point, Yukon, school playing at recess in the 1930s. *The General Synod Archives, Anglican Church of Canada, P9901-543.*

The Choutla school quickly developed a reputation for poor health (four students died of influenza in 1920, and more would die of tuberculosis and other diseases in coming years), harsh discipline, meagre diet, and unpleasant living quarters.[9] In 1923 Anglican Bishop Isaac Stringer wrote that "some of our best and most influential Indians object to sending their children away to school."[10] Not surprisingly, orphans and children from destitute families made up close to a third of the enrolment in most years.[11]

The church-run residential system grew slowly in the North, since the federal government resisted funding northern schools if there was no treaty obligation to provide schooling. By 1927 there were three Roman Catholic schools and one Anglican school in the Northwest Territories, a balance that did not change until the 1950s. In the Yukon, aside from the school at Carcross, the Anglicans opened a residence for Métis children in Dawson City in 1920, and ran a school for Inuit children at Shingle Point from 1929 to 1936. When this school closed, the students were transferred to the Anglican boarding school in the Northwest Territories.

In the Northwest Territories, the Catholics enjoyed more success among the Dene, while the Anglicans concentrated their efforts among the Inuit. There were conflicts within and between the schools on the basis of religion and ethnicity. Anthony Thrasher, a student at the Catholic school in Aklavik, was often in fights with students from the local Anglican school. "They picked on me for two things, because I was a Roman Catholic and because I was a damn Eskimo."[12]

The trip to a northern residential school could be long and lonely. In 1928 three children travelled from Herschel Island to the Anglican school at Hay River in the NWT. Ethel Catt, the missionary who accompanied them for part of the journey down the Mackenzie River, was distressed to discover that, when the time came to board the boat to take them down the river, one boy had run away and another refused to board. When they were all collected and put to bed, they burst into tears. Despite her best efforts, Catt was unable to comfort them. "I tried talking, singing, coaxing, but nothing would do & of course they did not know a word I said."[13] Travel was so difficult and arduous that parents of children sent to Carcross from more remote communities might not see them for a decade.[14]

Angela Sidney was one of the first students to attend Choutla. "When we first went over to that Choutla school, all those kids got off the cars, horse teams—we all started running around the Choutla school first. Oh, boy, lots of fun! We thought it was a good place we're going to stay.

Moravian Church and Mission School, Makkovik, Labrador. September 1926. *L.T. Burwash, Department of Indian Affairs and Northern Development collection, Library and Archives Canada, PA-099500.*

But that's the time we found out we couldn't even talk to our brothers! We got punished if we did. And we weren't supposed to talk Indian, Tlingit."[15]

Curriculum was left largely in the hands of the churches, and usually was limited to religious instruction, coupled with an introduction to reading and arithmetic. In 1913 federal inspector H.B. Bury worried that students left the schools poorly equipped for either white society or a return to their home communities. Parents and grandparents complained they had little control over returned students who had received little training in how to live on the land. For their part, many of the students felt ashamed of their home communities.[16]

Discipline could be harsh: in response to the theft of food in 1940, Choutla principal H.C.M. Grant had an offender beaten as an example. The boy, dressed in his pajamas, had to be held down on a desk by the matron and the farm instructor in front of all the other students. Grant said he then subjected the boy to a severe strapping.[17] Twenty years later, in the early 1960s, the entire boys' dormitory at Choutla was put to bed immediately after dinner for a month because no one would reveal which of the boys had been telling stories after lights out.[18]

Student labour was needed to operate the schools. In 1882 the Grey Nuns expressed concern over the amount of work the Oblates required of students at schools in the NWT.[19] At both the Anglican and Catholic schools, boys spent a half day gardening, fishing, or woodworking, and the girls prepared meals, cleaned the schools, and

> **"**
> *We couldn't even talk to our brothers! We got punished if we did. And we weren't supposed to talk Indian, Tlingit.*
> **"**
> Angela Sidney, former student

made and repaired clothing. The demand for fuel to feed the wood-burning stoves was constant during the long, cold winters, and wore out many children. Every fall, a

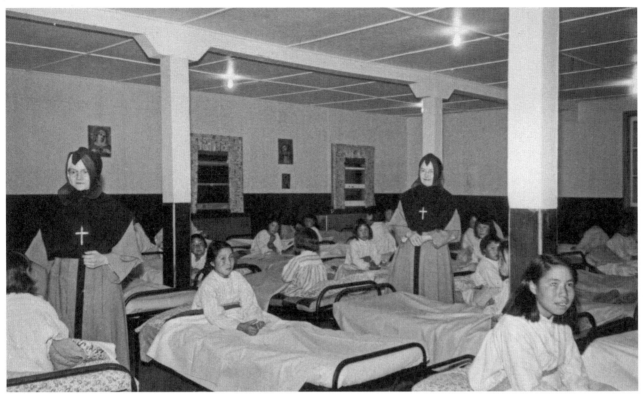

The girls' dormitory, Turquetil Hall, Chesterfield Inlet, Northwest Territories, 1958. *Library and Archives Canada, Charles Gimpel, Charles Gimpel fonds, PA-210885.*

barge would arrive in Aklavik, loaded with kindling for the school furnace. The students would form a long chain from the barge to the furnace room, and, with the assistance of the school staff, unload the barge.[20]

During the missionary period, enrolment in the northern residential schools was low. In a region with 2000 school-aged children, there were only fifty-nine students at Sacred Heart in Fort Providence in 1918.[21] By 1939 the federal government subsidized the education of approximately 30 percent of the school-aged First Nations children in the Mackenzie District of the NWT. Most of the students had been placed in residential schools because they were orphans or their families were judged to be destitute.[22] Although girls tended to remain in school for longer periods, for most students, schooling lasted only four or five years.[23] In 1948, while there were four residential schools in the NWT and three in the Yukon, most Aboriginal children in the North were not attending school regularly. In the NWT, 200 of the 300 students in residential schools were in the first or second grade.[24]

No residential schools were built in the Quebec portion of the Ungava peninsula. However, Moravian missionaries had been active in Nunatsiavut in Labrador since 1752. They established a boarding school, intended largely for Inuit students, in 1901.[25] In the 1920s, the International Grenfell Association, a Protestant missionary organization, opened the first of its boarding schools for children of all ancestries orphaned by the 1919 influenza epidemic.[26]

The New North

The creation of the department of Northern Affairs and National Resources in 1953 marked the beginning of the end of the period of direct missionary control over education in the North. At the time, there were eight different educational agencies in operation in the NWT alone, providing a very uneven patchwork of service. Some schools were open only for a few hours a day, and a third of the teachers lacked certification. The former federal Director of Northern Administration for Northern Affairs, R.A.J. Phillips, concluded there was "No policy, no curriculum for northern needs, and no training for northern teachers."[27]

Education was to be the new department's priority. There was concern that since the Aboriginal population in the North was growing, while fur revenues were in decline, coming generations of northerners would become

At the Coppermine Tent Hostel, which opened in 1955 in what is now Nunavut, students lived in wood-framed field tents. *The General Synod Archives, Anglican Church of Canada, P7530 (229).*

dependent on government assistance.[28] Education, it was argued, would give children the skills needed to succeed in the new North that government officials sought to bring into being. The fact that the family allowance, introduced during the Second World War, was paid only if school-aged children were in school provided an additional incentive for parents to enrol their children.[29] The federal government's goal was to provide every school-aged child in the North with the opportunity to go to school by 1968. To do this, it made a major investment in residential schooling. This decision by Northern Affairs to expand the residential school system in the North so dramatically was taken a decade after Indian Affairs officials had begun to wind down the system in southern Canada. Just as on the Prairies, residential school expansion in the North went hand-in-hand with intensified resource development and speculation, and an enhanced military presence.

Not only was the expansion of residential schooling in the North undertaken with virtually no consultation with Aboriginal people, according to J.G. Wright, Superintendent of Eastern Arctic Patrol, those northerners the government had spoken with had all agreed "it would be a grave mistake to transport native children any distance from their homes for education."[30] Government officials had not intended initially to replicate the church-run residential school system in the North. However, church opposition, coupled with the belief that residential schools would be cheaper, led them to abandon plans to rely solely on government-run community schools.[31]

During the missionary period, the federal government had turned down Roman Catholic proposals to establish a residential school in the Yukon. However, in 1950 it agreed to support a school in Lower Post, British Columbia, which was just below the Yukon-BC border, and drew many of its students from the territory. The Anglican school at Carcross was rebuilt and expanded in 1953. In 1960 the federal government built Anglican and Catholic residences for students attending day schools in Whitehorse, which had become the capital the Yukon in 1953. In addition, from the late 1940s until the early 1960s, a Baptist missionary society that originated in Alaska ran a small boarding school in Whitehorse.

From 1954 to 1964, Northern Affairs (rather than Indian Affairs, which was part of a different department at that time) opened four, large, day schools in the Northwest Territories: Chesterfield Inlet (1954), Yellowknife (1958), Inuvik (1959), and Fort Simpson (1960). In addition, it opened a vocational training school for Inuit in Churchill, Manitoba, in 1964. Most of the students who attended these schools were housed in new government-built residences (usually called "Halls"). These residences were to be managed by the Anglican and Catholic churches, which closed their old, run-down, residential schools. As a result, there were often two residences, one Anglican and one Catholic, in each community. In some cases, the school also had two wings—one for Catholics and one for Protestants. The exceptions were the Akaitcho Hall and the Sir John Franklin school in Yellowknife, and the Churchill Vocational Centre, which were operated by the

Yukon Hall, the Anglican residence in Whitehorse, Yukon. *Yukon Archives, Edward Bullen fonds, 82-354 #25.*

federal government on a non-denominational basis. All the schools were intended to be non-denominational, but it was decided to allow the Roman Catholics to operate the Sir Joseph Bernier school and Turquetil Hall residence in Chesterfield Inlet on Hudson Bay.[32]

Following a brief period of experimentation with tent hostels in 1951, the Coppermine Tent Hostel opened in 1955 in what is now Nunavut. The hostel was owned and funded by the federal government, and operated by the Anglican Church. The students lived in wood-framed field tents, and attended a federally funded day school in Coppermine. These tents were easy to build, but they were drafty, easily damaged by high winds, and difficult to heat. The hostel operated five months a year, and housed twenty to thirty students, most of whom were from the Coppermine area. In 1959 the hostel closed, and most students were transferred to Inuvik.

A series of smaller residences, usually referred to as "hostels," were established near settlements in the Northwest Territories and northern Quebec. At the hostels, the children lived with Inuit adults, who were often family members.[33] These smaller hostels could accommodate between eight and twenty-four students, who attended local federal day schools established throughout the North. Not all these hostels operated every year, and most were closed by the end of the 1960s.[34] Carolyn Niviaxie was an Inuit student from Sanikiluaq in what is now Nunavut, who went to a small hostel in Great Whale River (now Kuujjuarapik), Quebec. Niviaxie said that the hostel mother at Kuujjuarapik did not take good care of the

children, giving the food and clothing intended for the hostel children to her own family. "Every weekend we used to go to different relatives to do housecleaning, get water, like they used to have tanks for water, and getting water, carrying water until it was full, all day. We had different chores; one just to clean up the house, one just to get water, for different relatives, in different houses."[35]

Most students living in the residences were Aboriginal, but the northern schools and residences were not restricted to Aboriginal students.[36] Albert Canadien, who attended mission schools at Fort Providence and Fort Resolution, appreciated the diversity of students living in Yellowknife's Akaitcho Hall. "There, I lived and went to school with Inuit, Métis, white, and even Chinese students. This was quite a change for me from the residential school days. Living at [Akaitcho Hall] at that time proved to be a good experience for me in later life. It taught me to get along with and respect people from other cultures, to treat them like you would anyone else."[37]

From 1956 to 1963, there was a major increase in the number of Inuit youth attending both residential and day schools. In the eastern Arctic, for example, attendance rose from 201 to 1173, and from 1755 to 3341 in the western Arctic. In the Ungava district of northern Quebec, it jumped from 39 to 656.[38] This increase could not be accomplished without a dramatic intervention into the lives of Aboriginal people. In many communities, the arrival of a government-chartered airplane was the prelude to a traumatic scene in which intimidated parents

The Stringer Hall dining hall in 1970. Stringer Hall, in Inuvik, was one of the church-operated student residences the federal government built in the 1950s and 1960s. *Northwest Territories Archives, Wilkinson, N-1979-051: 0400s.*

bid farewell to frightened children, who were flown away to school.[39]

Unlike the missionaries, many of whom had learned to speak Aboriginal languages, most of the new teachers came from the South, spoke no Aboriginal language, and usually had no more than one or two days of orientation for living in the North. Few stayed for more than two years.[40] At Inuvik, seventeen of thirty-four teachers resigned in 1960. The following year, fifteen of thirty-five teachers resigned, and in 1962 sixteen of thirty-four resigned.[41]

Director of Northern Administration for Northern Affairs R.A.J. Phillips said that the department, which viewed itself as the most effective protector of Eskimo (the term used at that time) culture, was prepared to use local languages in the lower grades. But, because a liberal education could be achieved only through the use of a major language, the department was committed to using English as the language of instruction.[42] Indeed, since few teachers spoke anything but English, it could hardly be otherwise.[43] Languages did not have to be banned to be lost. In 1959 the father of an Inuit boy wrote to the Inuvik school that his son had gone to school with a fluent command of his native language. But, in a recent letter home, he had written, "I am forgetting how to write in Eskimo now as we are only taught in English." This news, he said, had left his mother, who only knew Inuktitut, heartbroken. The Anglican hostel director responded that while English

was the language of instruction, children at his school were not punished for speaking their language. However, he thought the best solution would be for the mother to learn English.[44]

In 1958 two Inuit teaching assistants were hired. By 1968 thirty-seven assistants worked in the system.[45] A plan to educate Inuit children in their own language from Kindergarten to Grade 3 was not in place until the early 1970s.[46]

Like the teachers, the curriculum came from the South: most schools used the Alberta, Manitoba, or Ontario curricula. For many students, the resulting education was difficult, irrelevant, and frustrating. At the Catholic School at Akalavik, Lillian Elias could not relate to the world presented in her readers. "When I looked at Dick and Jane, I thought Dick and Jane were in heaven when I saw all the green grass. That's how much I knew about Dick and Jane."[47]

Jack Anawak, an Inuk who attended school at Chesterfield Inlet, and who went on to become a Member of Parliament, recalled, "We were dealt with in a herd, never as individuals, never being able to speak the only language we ever knew. Punishments were inflicted that were beyond anything Inuit could have ever imagined could be done to a child. Our way of life was denigrated; our beliefs and values were constantly trashed; our spirituality was challenged only to be replaced by the God people, with a consistently cruel, unrelenting depravity, the likes of which other Canadians cannot imagine."[48]

The students often came from thousands of kilometres away. It was not uncommon for Inuit children from northern Quebec to travel for over a week by train and plane to get to school in Yellowknife in the Northwest Territories. Often, neither the parents nor the children knew where they were going. There was no way for parents to visit, or for students to return home for holidays. Two of the sons of Apphia Agalakti Siqpaapik Awa, an Inuit woman from the eastern High Arctic, were sent to school in Churchill. "We couldn't communicate with them because there were no phones, and since we were in the camp, we didn't get any letters from them. We didn't hear from them for a long, long time. We didn't know how they were down there. I remember being so worried about them."[49] The impact on the communities remained disruptive. In 1972 Nashook, an Inuit man from Pond Inlet, said the children who returned from the schools "loathe their culture and look down on the old ways of their parents."[50]

Overcrowding was common in the new residences. Not long after it opened, the Chesterfield Inlet facility, built for eighty, had a population of one hundred.[51] Efforts to ease overcrowding by sending children to other schools were complicated by the principal's insistence that Catholic children not be housed with Protestant children.[52] After giving consideration to an expansion, federal officials solved crowding problems in Yellowknife by tightening admission requirements.[53] In Inuvik by 1962, 850 students were attending a facility designed for 600. The students slept in open-area dormitories with no privacy. Parents petitioned Ottawa for improvements, administrators warned that enrolment was expected to hit 960 in 1965, but the federal government simply added makeshift classrooms.[54] In these crowded conditions, staff were stressed and overworked. In 1964 problems such as understaffing and a lack of time off caused the entire staff in Churchill to threaten to quit en masse.[55] The domestic education the students received was of limited use, since the foods they were taught to prepare often were not available in the North or were very expensive. Similarly, at a time when most families were using oil-fired stoves, students were taught to cook on electric stoves.[56]

Overall, the federal system never met its goals. As late as 1967, 20 percent of the Inuit population was without educational opportunity.[57] In the last part of the 1960s, the federal government transferred most of the

schools, the residences, and responsibility to the territorial governments.

Until the 1960s, the Yukon and NWT were governed by appointed officials, most of whom lived in Ottawa. For example, it was not until 1967 that the NWT's administrative offices were moved from Ottawa to Yellowknife. The creation of a fully elected assembly came even later.[58] As northerners gained control over their governments, support for residential schooling declined, and support for local schooling increased.[59]

In Yukon, the Carcross school closed in 1969. The Roman Catholic Coudert Hall in Whitehorse merged with the Anglican Yukon Hall two years later, and Yukon Hall

> **"**
> *We didn't hear from them for a long, long time. We didn't know how they were down there. I remember being so worried about them.*
> **"**
> Apphia Agalakti Siqpaapik Awa, parent

itself remained in operation until 1985. The Lower Post, British Columbia, school closed in 1975.

In the Northwest Territories, the three Anglican residences all were closed by the mid-1970s. Roman Catholic involvement with Grollier Hall in Inuvik continued until 1987. The residence was operated for another nine years by the territorial government. After being transferred to the government in 1972, Lapointe Hall in Fort Simpson was turned over to the Aboriginal Koe Go Cho society, and eventually taken over by the Deh Cho Aboriginal Council. Breynat Hall in Fort Smith was closed in 1975 after a fire. The non-denominational Akaitcho Hall closed in 1994.

In the eastern Arctic (now Nunavut), most of the hostels had closed by the end of the 1960s. The exceptions were in Cambridge Bay and Iqaluit. The Iqaluit school and residence were proposed first in 1961, but the plans were dropped, only to be revived, without community

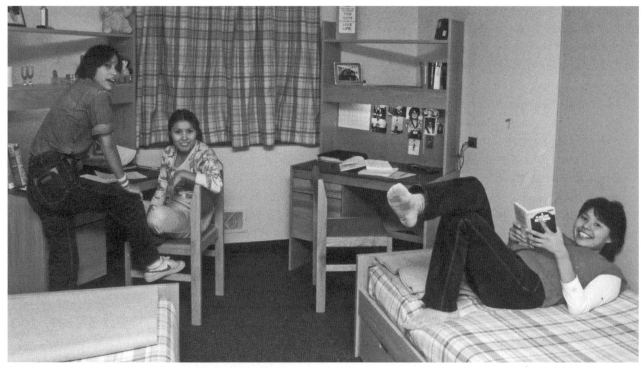

Students in a dormitory room in Akaitcho Hall in Yellowknife, Northwest Territories. *Northwest Territories Archives, Northwest Territories. Department of Public Works and Services, G-1995-001: 1605.*

consultation, in 1967. Construction began in 1969. At the time, teachers in smaller northern communities circulated petitions opposing the project. The project went ahead with both the school and residence—which had a capacity of 200—opening in 1971. In its early years, the school and the residence had difficulty attracting and keeping students. In 1973 school enrolment was one hundred, and only sixty students were in residence.[60] The hostel remained in operation until 1996, when it and the Cambridge Bay hostel both closed.

By the 1990s, former students had begun to speak out about the abuse they had experienced at a number of residential schools. Former employees of Coudert Hall in the Yukon, Lower Post in northern British Columbia, and Grollier Hall in the Northwest Territories were convicted of a variety of offences, including indecent assault. A 1994 territorial government report concluded that students at Turquetil Hall in Chesterfield Inlet had been subjected to serious sexual and physical abuse. Due in large measure to the passage of time, no charges ever were laid.[61]

While there were a number of successful schools, particularly Grandin College, overall, the federal government's record in running residential schools in northern Canada suggests it had learned little from its failures in the South. Children were separated from their parents, their communities, their languages, and their cultural

practices. Facilities were crowded, the lessons were inappropriate, teachers poorly prepared, and educational goals unclear.

As Salamiva Weetaluktuk reflected, the legacies were similar as well: "Nobody is making the connection. Bad Indians, Bad Inuit. Drunken Inuit. Drunken Indians. That's all they think. But we would not be drunken Inuit or drunken Indians had we not been abused when we were children, had we not been exposed to assault and stuff like that."[62]

While the system was late in coming to the North, its impact was significant, and continues to the present. A far higher percentage of the Aboriginal population in northern Canada attended residential schools than was the case in the rest of Canada. According to the 2001 Statistics Canada Aboriginal Peoples Survey, over 50 percent of Aboriginal people forty-five years of age and older in Yukon and the Northwest Territories attended a residential school. In Nunavut 40 percent of those fifty-five and older attended residential school as did over 50 percent of those aged forty-five to fifty-four.[63] The impact is compounded by the fact that Aboriginal people constitute a majority or near majority throughout northern Canada.

CHAPTER FOUR

The Experience of the Métis and Residential Schools

Two Métis children with an Inuit child at the Shingle Point, Yukon, school, 1930. *J.F. Moran, Department of Indian Affairs and Northern Development fonds, Library and Archives Canada, 1973-357; a102086.*

During his inspection of the Native American boarding school system in the United States in 1879, Nicholas Flood Davin had been impressed by the role that people of mixed ancestry played in the operation of the schools. He concluded that Métis could serve as the "natural mediator between the Government and the red man, and also his natural instructor." He recommended that the federal government educate the Métis along with First Nations people in "self-reliance and industry" in industrial schools.[1] The Oblate missionaries also sought to use the Métis as a bridge between the two cultures. This was one reason why Bishop Alexandre Taché sent Louis Riel and two other young Métis to Montreal for additional education at a seminary in 1858.[2] Riel never taught at a Canadian residential school, but he did teach Métis children at a Jesuit boarding school in Montana in the 1880s.[3] Riel's sister Sara was a Grey Nun who taught at a residential school in Île-à-la-Crosse in what is now Saskatchewan from 1871 until her death in 1883.[4] This, however, was not the normal residential school experience for Métis people.

The Métis nation emerged out of the fur trade when traders and Aboriginal women established long-lasting relationships, and raised families. Early Métis communities appeared around the Great Lakes, and moved west with the fur trade.[5] When the Hudson's Bay Company and the North-West Company merged in 1821, numerous trading posts closed, and many of their Métis employees moved to Red River, which evolved into a centre for a Métis culture with distinct values, forms of organizations, arts, and language.[6]

The Métis played central roles in both the Red River Resistance of 1870 and the Northwest Rebellion of 1885. In 1870 their efforts led to the creation of Manitoba as a province, and the provision of 1.4 million acres of land to be distributed to the children of Métis families. The gains were short-lived: speculators dispossessed many of the Métis; and settlers from Ontario treated the Manitoba Métis with disdain, sometimes subjecting them to violent attacks. By 1885 over three quarters of the Métis population of Manitoba had left for what is now Saskatchewan and Alberta.[7] Métis communities also developed in the North and the West in places such as the Mackenzie River Valley.[8] Following the defeat of the 1885 rebellion, which was sparked by government failure to address Métis concerns over land, the federal government executed Riel, and much of the Métis leadership was dispersed.

The churches often accepted Métis children into residential schools, but the federal government preferred to limit its support to status Indians. Funding Métis students, from Ottawa's perspective, was too costly, unnecessary (since the Métis often were Christian and considered "sufficiently civilized"), and, ultimately, not the federal government's responsibility. The policy was not applied consistently. Initially, schools were allowed to take in Métis children when there were empty beds, if parents were prepared to pay, or if Indian Affairs had determined that the parents were living "as Indians."[9] This term was broad enough to include living on a reserve, hunting and trapping, or living in conditions of severe poverty.[10]

After 1885, as Euro-Canadian immigrants settled the West, the Métis were increasingly marginalized, living in shantytowns on the edges of town or just outside reserves. Few had the money to take up farming, and many relied on manual labour, such as freighting, lumbering, collecting buffalo bones, harvesting roots, and hunting and trapping, to survive.[11] Most of their communities lacked the finances to build schools, and public schools often were unwilling to admit Métis children.[12] A

In 1884 Louis Riel worked as a teacher at the Jesuit St. Peter's Mission boarding school for Métis in Sun River, Montana. In June 1884, he wrote that "My health suffers from the fatiguing regularity of having to look after children from six in the morning until eight at night, on Sunday as well as on the days of the week." *Saskatchewan Archives Board, R-A2305.*

1936 commission on Métis people in Alberta concluded that 80 percent of Métis children were not in school.[13] For those parents who wanted to see their children educated, the only option was to try to have them accepted in a residential school.[14]

Anglican and Catholic missionaries sometimes were moved to establish schools in an effort to convert Métis parents and children to their faith. The Oblates, for example, established schools in Fort Providence and Fort Chipewyan, Alberta, to provide Métis fur-trade employees with an alternative to sending their children to Anglican schools.[15] In some cases, Catholic Métis parents who sent their children to Anglican schools were excommunicated.[16] When Treaty 8 was negotiated in 1899, Oblate missionaries encouraged Métis parents to declare themselves Indians rather than Métis. This would allow them

Students with Bishop Isaac Stringer in front of St. Paul's Hostel in Dawson, Yukon, 1923. Most of the students living at the hostel were Métis.
Yukon Archives, Isaac and Sadie Stringer fonds, 82/332, #28.

to send their children to residential school—and the church to collect a subsidy from the federal government.[17]

Oblate Father Albert Lacombe at the High River school in Alberta, and Father Joseph Hugonnard at the Qu'Appelle, Saskatchewan, school were among the many residential school principals who recruited Métis students. They were acting both out of concern for the educational needs of Métis children and in response to the problems they were having in convincing First Nation parents to send their children to residential school. The federal government insisted that Métis parents pay $155 a year to send their children to High River.[18] In 1912, much to the frustration of the deputy minister of Indian Affairs, sixty-six Métis students were admitted to the school.[19]

In 1913 Indian Affairs gave the Qu'Appelle school a year to replace fifty-one Métis students with First Nation students. Two years later, thirty of the Métis students were still there. In following years, Indian Affairs refused to admit Métis students who did not have status under the *Indian Act*.[20]

The federal government regularly tightened and loosened its Métis admission policy in the system's early years. Concerns about costs were constantly being balanced against worries that the Métis, without education,

would become a public menace. For example, in 1899, Indian Affairs minister Clifford Sifton argued in favour of admitting all children who lived on reserves to the residential schools, since the schools had been "instituted in the public interest, so that there should not grow up upon reserves an uneducated and barbarous class."[21] Arguing in the same vein, Qu'Appelle principal Hugonnard warned that the Métis could become a danger to the community if they were not educated, and he attempted to have potential students added to band lists.[22]

By the 1920s, the federal admissions policy for Métis began to tighten permanently. In 1924 Indian Affairs Commissioner W.A. Graham reported that with hard work, he had "got every child out of the Qu'Appelle school who had no right to be there."[23] In 1934 the word from Ottawa was that "absolutely no half-breed children can be admitted to our schools."[24] In practice, the churches might still admit Métis children, but the federal government would subsidize them only in extreme cases.

The Roman Catholic and Anglican churches operated at least three residential schools largely for Métis children: Île-à-la-Crosse in Saskatchewan, Saint-Paul-des-Métis in Alberta, and St. Paul in the Yukon.

Life was difficult for the teachers and the Métis students at the Île-á-la-Crosse school in the 1870s. The school matron slept on a pallet in the classroom, the female students slept on the floor, while the male students slept in the Oblate residence. *Glenbow Archives; PD-353-22 [ca. 1913-1914] Photographer, Thomas Waterworth.*

In 1846 an Oblate mission had been established at Île-à-la Crosse, in what is now Saskatchewan. From 1860 to 1996, Grey Nuns provided a range of educational and health services there, including a residential school for Métis children. Non-Métis children were sent to the Roman Catholic residential school at nearby Beauval.[25] By 1871 there were twenty-six students in their boarding school, along with five orphans who were being cared for by the Grey Nuns.[26] Initially, the education at the school was in French, but on her arrival in the early 1870s, Sara Riel introduced English lessons. The Métis opposed the education of their children in English, and demanded that the school be closed. Instead, the English classes were dropped.[27] In 1874 conditions at the school were so dire that the Grey Nuns had to ask parents to take their children back temporarily because they could not feed them.[28]

Alphonse Janvier, who attended Île-à-la Crosse for five years, described it in terms very similar to those used by students of other residential schools. For example, the sexes were strictly segregated. "We were not allowed to intermingle with the females, and many of them that were there had some nieces or nephews. You were not allowed to talk to them because this playground had an imaginary boundary that we could not cross."[29]

In 1896 Saint-Paul-des-Métis was established by Father Lacombe as a colony for landless Métis in what is now Alberta. The federal Department of the Interior provided a one-time grant of $2000. When Indian Affairs refused to fund a residential school, the Oblates held a fundraising campaign for a three-storey school that opened in 1903. Angered by what they saw as the school's harsh discipline, students set the school on fire in 1905. The fire destroyed the entire school, and left one child dead. The school's destruction marked the beginning of the end of Saint-Paul as a Métis community. By 1908 the federal government decided to terminate the colony, with the blessing of the Board of Management of Saint-Paul-des-Métis, but without consultation with the Métis.[30] In the following years, most of the Métis who had settled there were displaced by non-Aboriginal settlers.

The Anglican Church established the St. Paul's residence for Métis children in a private home in Dawson City, Yukon, in 1920. Their parents paid fees to support the residence, and the church and local businesses also made financial contributions. The residence was relocated to a former hospital in 1923 and closed in 1952.[31]

Aside from these three, in the 1950s the Alberta government began placing (and paying for) Métis children who had been apprehended by child welfare authorities in residential schools. The Grouard school, in particular, took in a large number of Métis students during this period.[32] The results of an inspection of the Grouard school by a provincial government psychiatrist in 1958 was so disturbing that the province stopped sending children to the school.[33]

> "
> *We weren't allowed to speak Cree, only French and English, and for disobeying this, I was pushed into a small closet with no windows or light, and locked in for what seemed like hours.*
> "
>
> Maria Campbell, former student

The Métis experience in the residential schools was similar to that of other Aboriginal children: poor food, harsh discipline, hard work, and a limited education. In 1914 a Métis woman complained that her children at the High River residential school had gone without boots for three months. That same year, a Saskatchewan lawyer, Arthur Burnett, wrote the department on behalf of a Métis man who complained the High River principal would not let him take his children out of the school for the summer.[34] Métis writer Maria Campbell was seven years old when she was sent to the Beauval residential school in Saskatchewan, largely at the instigation of her grandmother. "We weren't allowed to speak Cree, only French and English, and for disobeying this, I was pushed into a small closet with no windows or light, and locked in for what seemed like hours." She did not return after that first

year because a day school had opened near her parents' home.[35]

Raphael Ironstand, a Métis boy from western Manitoba, attended the Pine Creek school, where he was bullied by Cree boys. "They called me 'Monias,' while telling me the school was for Indians only. I tried to tell them I was not a Monias, which I now knew meant white man, but a real Indian. That triggered their attack, in unison. I was kicked, punched, bitten, and my hair pulled out by the roots. My clothes were also shredded, but the Crees suddenly disappeared, leaving me lying on the ground, bleeding and bruised." According to Ironstand, the nuns refused to believe his story, and forced him to mend his clothing.[36]

While it was not unusual for many students to spend a decade in the schools and emerge with only a Grade 2 standing, Archie Larocque, who did not start school at Fort Resolution until his late teens, was grateful for the opportunity to get any education. "They knew I was only going to be there for that one term because I was over the age limit. So they drove all they could into me."[37] In some cases, Métis parents placed their children in residential school because they could not afford to care for them. But there were also instances of parents undergoing considerable sacrifice to pay for their children's education. James Thomas, who went to the St. Bernard school for ten years, recalled that it took all the money his father earned to send his children to school.[38] Angie Crerar, who attended Fort Resolution, said the only positive memories she had of residential school were the friendships she formed with other students. "We tried to look after the little ones and tried to avoid some of the beatings that were not necessary. There was no such thing as respect but we taught ourselves to have respect."[39]

As is the case with many aspects of the residential school story, there is still much to be learned about the experience of Métis people in the residential schools. In particular, there is more to be learned about the degree to which their experiences, and the legacy of those experiences, differ from those of First Nations and Inuit students.

CHAPTER FIVE

The Staff Experience

Staff and students of the Coqualeetza, British Columbia, school in the late nineteenth century. *The United Church of Canada Archives, 93.049P411N. (18--?)*

For most of the system's history, residential school staff worked long hours for low pay, in locations isolated from their families and home communities. Just as the students were denied holidays, they often were denied holidays. Just as the students put up with unhealthy living conditions, the teachers lived in comparatively spartan settings. They rarely were given the tools to care for children properly, let alone teach them. Many of the positive aspects of the residential school system, then, were the result of their creativity and ingenuity. As a group, they were part of a colonial process that employed a harsh discipline to suppress Aboriginal culture. On the individual level, many were dedicated and made real contributions. Many were young people in search of employment and adventure, with little idea of what lay ahead of them.

Until the 1950s, the churches took the primary responsibility for hiring school staff. For teachers, the Catholics drew from a number of female religious orders, whose recruits were often young women from rural backgrounds. The Missionary Oblate Sisters, based in St. Boniface, for example, taught in prairie schools. More than half the Oblate sisters recruited between 1904 and 1915, a period of considerable growth for the small order, came from

Quebec. The world these young women entered was governed by rules and the need for obedience. They had to give up their names, their clothing, and personal belongings (as one sister recalled, even a little thimble given to her as a present had to be sacrificed). They were discouraged from developing close friendships (which could be divisive within a small organization), and encouraged to take their religious direction from priests. Relations with people outside the order were regulated, and the directress read any letters they sent or received. Meals could be skimpy. Asking for more food was frowned upon, but, at the same time, one was expected to eat everything put on one's plate.[1] It was from this experience of personal sacrifice, intense commitment, and obedience that they went forward to teach in residential schools.

The Protestant churches hired staff on the basis of their Christian zeal.[2] One applicant for a position with a Presbyterian school wrote, "I have for four years felt called to devote my life, for the extension of His kingdom amongst the heathen, and He has especially given me a strong desire to spend all the rest of my years amongst the heathen here in my own beloved native land."[3]

T.B. Marsh, the principal of the Hay River, Northwest Territories, school, with school staff and students. *The General Synod Archives, Anglican Church of Canada, P8001 (29).*

It would be a mistake to think that all the teachers were unqualified. There were, for example, a number of well-trained women who worked at schools in the North in the early twentieth century. Among the Anglicans, Louise Topping had trained as a teacher and a nurse; Adelaide Butler had taught for nine years in England before going to work in Shingle Point; Mabel Jones, another Shingle Point teacher, had a degree in theology; and Margaret Peck, who taught in Aklavik, had a degree from Oxford.[4] A study of the staff at four Presbyterian schools in Saskatchewan, Manitoba, and northwestern Ontario from 1888 to 1923 found that a third of the twenty-four principals who worked at the schools during that period had university degrees.[5] In the 1954–1955 school year, eighty teachers at all government-funded Indian day and residential schools had university degrees. A decade later, the number had increased to 228 (or 15.5 percent of the total teaching staff).[6]

There were people who committed much of their lives to residential school work. Annie McLaren was the matron of the Birtle, Manitoba, school for twenty-five years. Jeanie Gilmour was the Crowstand, Saskatchewan,

matron for fifteen years. Reverend W.A. Hendry was principal of the Portage la Prairie school for over thirty years.[7] But these examples of long service were the exception. A study of four prairie schools showed that from 1888 to 1923, the average stay of a teacher was three years, and for principals, it was five and a half years.[8] In 1963, of the five teachers at the Carcross school in the Yukon, only one had been there for more than a year.[9] As late as 1964, the annual staff turnover rate for all government-run Indian schools was 29.3 percent.[10]

The Catholic schools had lower turnover rates, due in some measure to the vows of obedience taken by the members of religious orders. Paul Bousquet, the principal of the Fort Alexander school, discouraged by a continuing problem with runaways and ongoing conflicts with parents, tried unsuccessfully to resign in 1919. Even though he repeated the offer two years later, saying he was tired of working with Aboriginal children, the Oblates kept him on the job for another fourteen years, during which he served as principal at Fort Alexander, Fort Frances, and Camperville.[11]

Pupils and staff of the Fort Albany, Ontario, school in 1929. *Library and Archives Canada, Department of Indian Affairs and Northern Development fonds, C-068966.*

There were few limits on what might be required of the early school employees. The principal of a Presbyterian school in northwestern Ontario also served as missionary, steamboat captain, and farm instructor.[12] One Catholic principal could "run the farm, the plant, and all the outside work," but was judged as inadequate, because "the inside drudgery of cooking, mending, sewing, laundry work, taking care of the sick and a thousand other details do not register with him."[13]

Hours were long, days off rare, and responsibilities continuous. When the large and—for its time—modern Lejac school opened in 1922, Father Joseph Allard, who had been in charge of the much smaller Stuart Lake school, wrote of how relieved he was to have "finished the processions for half an hour every morning, rain, cold or shine, of 15 little boys, each one carrying pitchers of water for all the needs of a house filled with 80 people … finished the packing of wood for 14 stoves … finished the stove pipes that dripped soot on the floors and beds … finished the midnight errands with a stick in hand hitting the stove pipes red with heat to see if they held good together, fearing for the lives of 75 souls, his little ones,

sleeping in a fire trap."[14] Within a year of the opening of Lejac, Allard had a nervous breakdown, and had to resign as principal.[15]

Attitudes towards Aboriginal people and students changed over time. Furthermore, it is apparent that at any given time, different teachers took different approaches to their students. A change in principal could lead to a dramatic change in the school atmosphere.[16] While the comments of the teachers, particularly in the system's early years, reflected the stereotypes of the day regarding Aboriginal culture, they also expressed the view that their students were bright and capable.[17]

Many teachers were disheartened by their experience. Sarah LeRoy, who worked at Hay River in the Northwest Territories, commented, "The fight against the evil one has been hard, but still the joys of service have overbalanced the discouragements and disappointments."[18] Another teacher, writing from Carcross in the late 1920s, lamented she had "36 children to teach—from those who do not know one word of English and scream at the oppressiveness of a roof over their heads for the first time, to seniors in Grade Six."[19]

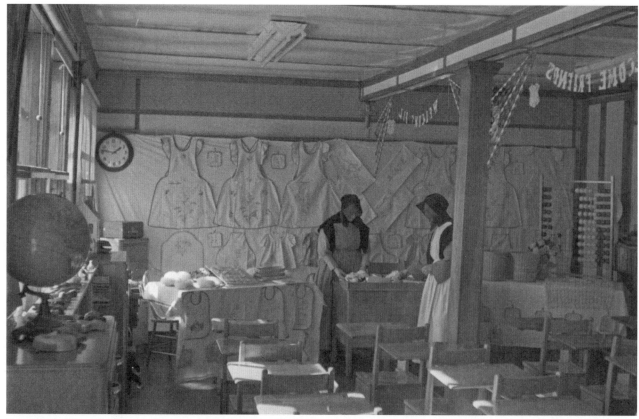

Nuns working on crafts at Immaculate Conception School in Aklavik, Northwest Territories, 1955. *Northwest Territories Archives, Wilkinson, N-1979-051: 1205.*

Teachers also spoke up on behalf of students. In 1911 a teacher at the St. George's school in Lytton, British Columbia, quit without giving notice, complaining in his letter of resignation of the way the principal was treating the students. The Anglican Church investigated, and fired the principal. Unfortunately, his replacement had a reputation for dictatorial behaviour.[20] Jennie Cunningham, a teacher at File Hills in Saskatchewan, wrote letters of complaint to both the federal government and the Presbyterian Church Foreign Mission Committee, pointing out that overcrowding was so bad that boys had been sleeping in tents for two years.[21]

While the teachers may have enjoyed better meals and more privacy than the students, theirs was a life of only comparative luxury. Sometimes, they were stricken with the same diseases that swept through the schools. Living in isolation with colleagues who were not necessarily of their own choosing could give rise to long-standing tensions. The principal of the Regina school had such a strong grip on his staff that he was able to forbid them to visit town.[22] For the Catholics, relations between religious orders were not always smooth: in 1890 a dispute with the Oblates led the Sisters of St. Ann to withdraw temporarily from the Kamloops school.[23]

Because the staff members were supposed to be motivated by religious commitment, they were expected to work for less money than other teachers. According to Hayter Reed, the deputy minister of Indian Affairs, the government expected that the churches would "engage employees at less wages than the Department and that they would keep within the allowance and reduce wages when necessary."[24] Payment was not always prompt: in the 1900s, a teacher at the Metlaktla school had not been paid for two years.[25] In addition, teachers often were expected to donate a portion of their wage back to the schools. From 1901 to 1904, Kate and Janet Gillespie donated a third of their income to the File Hills school.[26] The members of the Roman Catholic orders had taken vows of poverty and obedience. In some cases, their orders required them to work for room and board only. In other orders, such as the Sisters of Providence, who worked in Oblate-managed schools in the Athabasca region of Alberta, the sisters were paid $25 a year, plus room and board, by the Oblates.[27] The arrangement, struck in 1893, remained in place until 1955, when the sisters were allowed to receive the same salaries paid to Indian Affairs teachers. In exchange, the Oblates charged the sisters $40 a month for

In 1901 Kate Gillespie was appointed principal of the File Hills residential school. From 1901 to 1904, she donated a third of her income to the school. *Saskatchewan Archives Board, R-A4801.*

A class at the Alberni, British Columbia, school in the 1950s. *The United Church of Canada Archives, 93.049P428.*

room and board, and required them to pay for all their clothing, health, travel, and education costs.[28]

Friendships also developed between former students and school staff,[29] and many students retained positive memories about the impact of specific teachers.[30] Father Jean-Marie Pochat, the long-time principal of Grandin College in Fort Smith,[31] and Ralph Ritcey, the founder of the Churchill vocational school, for example, left lasting impressions. On the basis of a nomination from his former students, in 2005 Father Pochat was invested as a Member of the Order of Canada. Peter Irniq, then the Commissioner of Nunavut and a former student of Ritcey's, delivered the eulogy at Ritcey's funeral in 2003. Irniq described Ritcey as a man who "cared greatly about the future of Inuit, defended their rights and played a big part in eventually dismantling colonialism in the Arctic."[32]

There were a small number of Aboriginal teachers throughout the system's history. By 1858 three school graduates were teaching at the Alderville School at Alnwyck, Ontario.[33] Isaac Barefoot was hired to teach at his former school, the Mohawk Institute, in 1869.[34] In 1903 a Miss Cornelius, an Oneida woman who had attended industrial schools and teacher-training institutes in the United States, was teaching at the Regina school.[35]

Aboriginal staff members were not always made to feel welcome. When the principal of the Birtle, Manitoba, school married an Aboriginal woman who worked for the school, the couple faced opposition from other staff and the church, which transferred him to a different school.[36] In the 1940s, when the government attempted to have an Aboriginal man appointed principal of the Mohawk

Institute, the move was opposed successfully by the Anglican bishop, who suggested the difficult job of managing the school would be carried out more successfully "in hands other than those of an Indian, however well qualified he might be."[37]

Aboriginal people worked as the cleaning and maintenance staff in many schools, particularly after the half-day system was ended. Richard King, who taught at the Carcross school in the 1960s, wrote that these workers were usually former students, who, despite their interest in and knowledge of the students, were given few opportunities to interact with them.[38]

By the system's final years, some Aboriginal staff members were able to make a number of positive contributions to the retention and development of Aboriginal culture. Jose Kusugak, an Inuit leader who played a central role in the creation of Nunavut, was not only a former residential school student but a former teacher as well. While attending the Churchill vocational school, he concluded that education was central to Inuit cultural survival. Upon his graduation, he returned to the school as a cultural and language advisor. Eva Aariak, the premier of Nunavut, had Kusugak as a teacher in Churchill, and credits him for inspiring her "love of Inuit language and culture."[39]

CHAPTER SIX

The Continuing Legacy of Residential Schools

On her first sight of the Shingwauk school building in Sault Ste. Marie, Ontario, Jane Willis thought, "Nothing could ever go wrong in such beautiful surroundings." But a few months "was all it took to make me ashamed of the fact that I was Indian." Feelings of shame and inadequacy were part of the residential school system's ongoing legacy. *David Ewens Collection, Library and Archives Canada, PA-182262.*

Residential schools began to have an impact on Aboriginal people from the day the first child was enrolled. At the personal level, parents lost their children and children lost their parents. Parents and grandparents found that once they had been stripped of their responsibilities, their role in life was greatly diminished.

If the schools had operated for only one or two generations, the system's impact would have been far less destructive. Aboriginal people had been on this continent for thousands of years. They had developed their own distinct cultures, belief systems, laws, economies, and social organizations. These had allowed them to deal successfully with all manner of catastrophe. Initially, children returning from the schools could look to their extended families, and to healers and elders, for assistance in dealing with the trauma of residential schooling. As time went on, those elders and healers passed on. Some were not replaced, and in other cases, missionaries had undermined their role and position in society. Parents who had gone to residential school had themselves been damaged by the system. As a result, each generation of returning children had fewer and fewer resources upon which to draw.

The impacts began to cascade through generations, as former students—damaged by emotional neglect and often by abuse in the schools—themselves became parents. Family and individual dysfunction grew, until eventually, the legacy of the schools became joblessness,

Saskatchewan Aboriginal leaders John Tootoosis (left) and Edward Ahenakew (right) were among the many Aboriginal people who recognized early on the impact that residential schools were having on their students. *Saskatchewan Archives Board, R-A7662; R-B11359.*

poverty, family violence, drug and alcohol abuse, family breakdown, sexual abuse, prostitution, homelessness, high rates of imprisonment, and early death.[1]

Aboriginal observers were aware of the problems from the outset. Edward Ahenakew, who was born in 1885 and attended the Emmanuel College boarding school in Prince Albert, said that on leaving school, a student was "in a totally false position. He does not fit into the Indian life, nor does he find that he can associate with the whites. He is forced to act a part. He is now one thing, now another, and that alone can brand him as an erratic and unreliable fellow."[2] John Tootoosis, who went to the Delmas school in Saskatchewan from 1912 to 1916, said that "when an Indian comes out of these places it is like being put between two walls in a room and left hanging in the middle. On one side are all the things he learned from his people and their way of life that was being wiped out, and on the other side are the whiteman's ways which he could never fully understand since he never had the right amount of education and could not be part of it."[3]

These observations would not have been news to the federal government or the churches. Throughout the system's history, many bureaucrats, church leaders, and staff drew attention to the system's failings. In 1908 Samuel Blake, after conducting an investigation on behalf of the Anglican Church into its Aboriginal missionary work, concluded that day schools were preferable to boarding schools.[4] In 1923 Indian Commissioner W.A. Graham complained that former pupils were "more careless of their property and less able to manage their affairs and work than those Indians who have not attended school."[5] The government was aware that, even on its own terms, the system had been a failure from the outset. It failed to assimilate Aboriginal people, it failed to educate them in ways that would allow them to take control over their economic future, and it robbed them of their traditional skills. Samuel Gargan, a Dene man who went to residential schools in the 1950s and 1960s, went on to become Grand Chief of the Dehcho region of the Northwest Territories and a member of the NWT legislature. Despite these accomplishments, he regretted that "I was never able to reach my full potential as a hunter or trapper, an occupation that was supposed to be passed on to me by my father and mother."[6]

Tragically, the system was far more effective in accomplishing the destructive side of its mandate: the separation of children from their parents, their community, their language, their culture, and their spirituality.

Children missed their parents, but many also blamed them for sending them to residential school. One former student hated her parents for years "for abandoning me at the Indian school."[7] To one student, the most hurtful long-term effect was "the inability to show love to my mom, brothers, and sisters."[8] Although visits home provided a longed-for escape from the school, they were not without tension. In 1919 Sarah-Jane Essau, an Aboriginal woman from Moosehide in the Yukon, wrote that when children returned from residential school, "they won't have anything to do with us; they want to be with white people; they grow away from us."[9]

Marius Tungilik felt he had been taught "to hate our own people, basically, our own kind" while at school in Chesterfield Inlet. When he returned to Repulse Bay, he saw his community differently: "you begin to think and see your own people in a different light. You see them eating with their hands. You think, 'Okay, primitive.'"[10] Espérance, a woman who attended the Maliotenam school in Sept Isles, Quebec, found that "because we spoke so much French, when we returned home for the holidays, we couldn't speak our language anymore. That really isolated us from each other."[11]

Those who did graduate with employable skills often were excluded from work by employers who discriminated on the basis of race.[12] In other cases, their training did not meet existing needs, either because certain trades such as blacksmithing or typesetting were becoming obsolete, or because there was no regional demand for them.[13] The results were often poverty, frustration, and self-doubt. As Edward Ahenakew noted, the schools trained students to be obedient, rendering them passive. Harold Greyeyes said that while there was much that was positive about the Lebret school, "the one thing a student never questioned was a ruling of one of the staff. It just wasn't done and even after I left the school I found it very hard to question anything that came from an authority figure."[14]

The schools lacked the resources and capacity to provide children with affection. Alphonse Janvier could not recall "ever being hugged or ever being told that I was loved."[15] Deprived of affection and of their parents, many former students experienced tremendous difficulties in raising their own families. "When I had my four kids,

I never gave them hugs and I never told them I loved them."[16] Allan Mitchell said residential school taught him how not to love. "Because there was no affection shown. There was a lot of discipline. No affection, none whatsoever. I don't ever remember getting hugs from them, even on my birthdays or anything."[17] George Amato, who went to the St. Bernard school in Alberta for nine years, asked, "How are we supposed to know how to be a parent when you don't have any guidance from anybody? All I had in me all my life was anger."[18] Former Blue Quills student

> **"**
> *It visited us every day of our childhood through the replaying over and over of our parents' childhood trauma and grief which they never had the opportunity to resolve in their lifetimes.*
> **"**
>
> Vera Manuel, child of former students

Elise Charland said she was a terrible parent. "My children were growing up with my abusive behaviour of slapping, whipping, and screaming at them for everything they did. I loved them in a very sick way."[19] Although Vera Manuel and her brother did not attend residential school, "We didn't really escape it either as it visited us every day of our childhood through the replaying over and over of our parents' childhood trauma and grief which they never had the opportunity to resolve in their lifetimes."[20]

This massive disruption of Aboriginal families contributed to the "Sixties scoop"—the dramatic increase in the number of Aboriginal children apprehended by child welfare agencies in the 1960s and 1970s. By 1970 between 30 and 40 percent of the children in care were of Aboriginal status, even though Aboriginal people counted for only 4 percent of the population. Under this system, children not only were taken out of their families and home communities, but, to a significant extent, they were shipped out of the country. Many of the children responded to fostering and adoption in the same manner that previous generations had responded to residential schools: they ran away, they did poorly in school, and they grew up ashamed and confused about their heritage. Some were abused by their foster and adoptive parents; many turned to drugs, alcohol, crime, and suicide. In Manitoba, Edwin Kimmelman, the judge heading a provincial inquiry into Aboriginal child welfare, termed it "cultural genocide."[21]

The separation of the sexes and the strong emphasis on sin left many students confused about sexuality. As one woman put it, "We were never allowed to talk to boys because it was bad to talk to boys."[22] Another student said, "I believed sex was a sin so I couldn't enjoy the act, but I learned to be submissive, as I thought that's what I should be doing.[23] The confusion sometimes led to self-destructive behaviour. One former student said, "Girls became promiscuous, thinking this was the only way they could feel close to another person."[24]

Other students turned to alcohol and drugs. A former student said, "I was frustrated about how we were treated, humiliated, and degraded, so I drank and took drugs to numb the frustrations of how my life had turned out."[25] For many students, the problems compounded one on another.

Referring to one abusive principal, Salamiva Weetaluktuk, a former student from northern Quebec, said, "There are a few homeless people in Montreal because of that teacher, that principal."[26]

Those who were sexually and physically abused in the schools bore a particularly heavy burden. Just as the legacy of residential schooling continued long after the schools closed, the impact of abuse continues long after the abuse stops. Children recover best if they have the support of their family and community, something that was denied to residential school students. Many felt ashamed and isolated, some were prone to violence, and others went on to perpetuate the violence. For Ted Fontaine, an important moment came when he connected with a cousin who had been a few years ahead of him at the Fort Alexander school, and the two began to speak of their experiences. "When you live your whole life with the idea that you experienced something unnatural, and if you don't have an outlet or place to dump the garbage, you begin to wonder if it happened at all. I'm thankful that I found Chubb again. Otherwise my life may have

ended abruptly in some disastrous way or I may never have begun the work toward healing."[27]

From the early 1990s onward, former students have been working collectively to support each other, and to seek justice from the federal government and the churches. In 1991 the Caribou Tribal Council of Williams Lake, British Columbia, organized the First National Conference on Residential Schools. At that event, Bev Sellars, a former student, spoke of the need to break the cycle of pain and suffering the residential schools had initiated. She told delegates, "We cannot allow another generation to suffer from the past programming we received at the schools."[28] In British Columbia, the Indian Residential School Survivors Society was founded in

> ## "
> *We cannot allow another generation to suffer from the past programming we received at the schools.*
> "
> Bev Sellars, former student

1994.[29] The National Residential School Survivors' Society, founded in 2005, grew out of an informal gathering of residential school survivors groups in August 2003.[30] A community-based Aboriginal movement for healing and justice developed from the work of such groups.

In the 1990s, a series of class-action lawsuits were launched, leading in 2006 to the Indian Residential Schools Settlement Agreement, the largest class-action settlement in Canadian history. Ratified in 2007, the settlement included a compensation payment for any former residential school residents, based on verifying their attendance at a school listed in the settlement agreement. It also established an independent process under which those who suffered sexual or serious physical abuses, or other abuses that caused serious psychological effects, can receive additional compensation. Funding also was provided to the Aboriginal Healing Foundation to support initiatives that address the residential school legacy. The

Robert Joseph, an hereditary chief of the Gwa wa enuk First Nation, attended the Alert Bay, British Columbia, residential school for eleven years. Joseph was for many years the executive director of the BC-based Indian Residential School Survivors Society. The society supported former students and campaigned for public recognition of the history and impacts of the residential school system. *Fred Cattroll.*

In 1945, nine-year-old Nora Bernard, a Mi'kmaq child from Nova Scotia, was sent to the Shubenacadie school. She attended the school for five years. In 1995 she began organizing former residential school students. The class action lawsuit that arose from her work played an important role in leading to the Indian Residential Schools Settlement Agreement. *The Halifax Herald Ltd.*

settlement agreement also established a commemoration initiative, and the Indian Residential Schools Truth and Reconciliation Commission.

In the 1960s, Canadian churches began to examine their historical relationship with Aboriginal people. That led to their involvement in several campaigns in support of Aboriginal rights. In 1986 the United Church of Canada issued an apology for its attempts to impose European culture and values on Aboriginal people. As the Aboriginal survivor movement grew, apologies specific to the operation of residential schools came from the Roman Catholic Oblate Conference of Canada in 1991, from the Anglican Church of Canada in 1993, the Presbyterian Church in Canada in 1994, and the United Church in 1998.

On June 11, 2008, the Conservative Prime Minister of Canada, Stephen Harper, issued an apology to former residential students on behalf of all Canadians. Present on the floor of the House of Commons for this historic event were the Aboriginal leadership of Canada along with a number of former students. In his statement, the prime minister recognized that the primary purpose of the schools was to remove children from their homes and

families in order to assimilate them better into the dominant culture. Harper said, "These objectives were based on the assumption Aboriginal cultures and spiritual beliefs were inferior and unequal. Indeed, some sought, as it was infamously said, 'to kill the Indian in the child.' Today, we recognize that this policy of assimilation was wrong, has caused great harm, and has no place in our country."[31]

The prime minister was joined by the leaders of the other parties represented in the House of Commons, who also offered apologies for the role that the federal government had played in this shared history. The Liberal Leader of the Opposition, Stéphane Dion, acknowledged that the government's policy had "destroyed the fabric of family in First Nations, Métis and Inuit communities. Parents and children were made to feel worthless. Parents and grandparents were given no choice. Their children were stolen from them."[32] Bloc Québécois leader Gilles Duceppe asked Canadians to "picture a small village, a small community. Now picture all of its children, gone. No more children between seven and sixteen playing in the lanes

Canada's Aboriginal leaders along with a number of former residential school students were present on the floor of the House of Commons for the 2008 Residential School Apology. Clockwise from the left: former student Don Favel; former student Mary Moonias; former student Mike Cachagee, President of the National Residential School Survivors Society; former student Crystal Merasty; former student Peter Irniq; Patrick Brazeau, National Chief of the Congress of Aboriginal Peoples; Mary Simon, President of the Inuit Tapiriit Kanatami; Phil Fontaine, National Chief of the Assembly of First Nations; Beverley Jacobs, President of the Native Women's Association of Canada; Clem Chartier, President of the Métis National Council. Former student Marguerite Wabano is obscured by Phil Fontaine's headdress. *Canadian Press: Fred Chartrand.*

or the woods, filling the hearts of their elders with their laughter and joy."[33]

New Democratic Party leader Jack Layton pointed to the fact that the country was still living with the residential school legacy, and called on Canadians to help "reverse the horrific and shameful statistics afflicting Aboriginal populations, now: the high rates of poverty, suicide, the poor or having no education, overcrowding, crumbling housing, and unsafe drinking water. Let us make sure that all survivors of the residential schools receive the recognition and compensation that is due to them."[34]

In his response, Phil Fontaine, National Chief of the Assembly of First Nations, said the apology marked a new dawn in the relationship between Aboriginal people and the rest of Canada. Together, he said, Canadians could "achieve the greatness our country deserves. The apology today is founded upon, more than anything

else, the recognition that we all own our own lives and destinies, the only true foundation for a society where peoples can flourish."[35] Patrick Brazeau, National Chief of the Congress of Aboriginal Peoples, spoke of what he had learned from the former students, saying, "Because of your resiliency, your courage and your strength, you have made me the strong Aboriginal Algonquin Canadian that I am today, as you have others across this great land of ours."[36] Mary Simon, President of the Inuit Tapiriit Kanatami, pointed out that in tackling the hard work that remained to be done, "We need the help and support of all thoughtful Canadians and our governments to rebuild strong and healthy families and communities."[37] Clem Chartier, President of the Métis National Council, noted that he had attended a residential school, and pointed out that many issues regarding the relationship between Métis people and residential schools still are not resolved.

He said, "I hope and I do believe sincerely in the words of the minister that we will address this."[38] Beverley Jacobs, President of the Native Women's Association of Canada, spoke of how Aboriginal communities were recovering their traditions. "Now we have our language still, we have our ceremonies, we have our elders, and we have to revitalize those ceremonies and the respect for our people not only within Canadian society but even within our own peoples."[39]

Given that for most of the last century, the residential school story was perhaps the least-known dimension of Canadian history, these apologies are of historic importance. In the same month they were issued, the Truth and Reconciliation Commission took office. The Commission's mandate is extensive (and is reproduced in Appendix A of this document), but its overarching mission is to tell Canadians about the history of residential schools and the impact those schools have had on Aboriginal peoples, and to guide a process of national reconciliation. The appointment of this Commission marks not the end of the residential school story, but recognition by a growing number of Canadians of the need to address the relationship between Aboriginal and non-Aboriginal Canada. Most importantly, it marks a growing understanding of the opportunities that such a relationship can create for the whole country.

Conclusions

The information in this book is based largely on published material. Future Truth and Reconciliation Commission reports will make more extensive use of statements that Canadians are providing to the Commission on their involvement and understanding of residential schools. The Commission also will make use of new research. That work will provide all Canadians with a fuller and deeper understanding of the schools and their legacy. It also will outline the Commission's recommendations on how the ongoing process of reconciliation should continue.

There can be no movement toward reconciliation, however, without an understanding of the rationale, operation, and overall impact of the schools. Through its work, the Commission has reached certain conclusions about the residential school system. As stated in the introduction, the truth about the residential school system will cause many Canadians to see their country differently. These are hard truths, but only by coming to grips with these truths can we lay the foundation for reconciliation.

The Commission has concluded that:

1) Residential schools constituted an assault on Aboriginal children.
2) Residential schools constituted an assault on Aboriginal families.
3) Residential schools constituted an assault on Aboriginal culture.
4) Residential schools constituted an assault on self-governing and self-sustaining Aboriginal nations.
5) The impacts of the residential school system were immediate, and have been ongoing since the earliest years of the schools.
6) Canadians have been denied a full and proper education as to the nature of Aboriginal societies, and the history of the relationship between Aboriginal and non-Aboriginal peoples.

1) Residential schools constituted an assault on Aboriginal children.

- The residential school system separated children from their parents without providing them with adequate physical or emotional care or supervision.
- Due to this lack of care and supervision, the schools often were sites of institutionalized child neglect, excessive physical punishment, and physical, sexual, and emotional abuse.
- Persistent underfunding left the schools dependent on student labour.
- Several generations of children were traumatized by their residential school experience: by having been abused, by having witnessed abuse, or by having been coerced to participate in abuse.
- All these factors contributed to high mortality rates, poor health, and low academic achievement.

2) Residential schools constituted an assault on Aboriginal families.

- The residential school system was established with the specific intent of preventing parents from exercising influence over the educational, spiritual, and cultural development of their children.
- The schools not only separated children from their parents and grandparents, but because of the strict separation of girls from boys, they also separated sisters from brothers. Older siblings were also separated from younger siblings.
- As each succeeding generation passed through the system, the family bond weakened, and, eventually, the strength and structure of Aboriginal family bonds were virtually destroyed.
- Given the high mortality rates that prevailed for much of the system's history, many parents spent their lives grieving, never having been given a proper description of how their child died or where they were buried, and not being able to hold an appropriate ceremony of mourning.

3) Residential schools constituted an assault on Aboriginal culture.

- The residential school system was intended to "civilize" and "Christianize" Aboriginal children, replacing Aboriginal cultural values with Euro-Canadian values.
- The residential school system belittled and repressed Aboriginal cultures and languages. By

making students feel ashamed of who they were, the system undermined their sense of pride and self-worth. This deprived them of the cultural and economic advantages and benefits that come from knowing two languages.

4) **Residential schools constituted an assault on self-governing and self-sustaining Aboriginal nations.**

- The residential school system was intended to assimilate Aboriginal children into broader Canadian society. With assimilation would come the breaking up of the reserves and the end of treaty obligations. In this way the schools were part of a broader Canadian policy to undermine Aboriginal leaders and Aboriginal self-government.

5) **The impacts of the residential school system were immediate, and have been ongoing since the earliest years of the schools.**

- The damage extended far beyond the numbers of children who attended these schools: families, communities, and cultures all suffered. Students were estranged from their families and communities; cultural, spiritual, and language transmission was disrupted; education did not prepare children for traditional lifestyles or emerging economic opportunities (which often were limited); parenting skills were lost; and patterns of abuse were developed that continue to have an impact on communities today.
- The schools' legacy shaped people's whole life experience, including their employment and their interactions with social service agencies, the legal system, and the health care system. The system's impact does not stop with the survivors; it affects their interactions with their children and grandchildren—the intergenerational survivors. The impact of the schools is felt in every Aboriginal community in the country.

6) **Canadians have been denied a full and proper education as to the nature of Aboriginal societies, and the history of the relationship between Aboriginal and non-Aboriginal peoples.**

- Canadians generally have been led to believe—by what has been taught and not taught in schools—that Aboriginal people were and are uncivilized, primitive, and inferior, and continue to need to be civilized. Canadians have been denied a full and proper education as to the nature of Aboriginal societies. They have not been well informed about the nature of the relationship that was established initially between Aboriginal and non-Aboriginal peoples and the way that relationship has been shaped over time by colonialism and racism. This lack of education and misinformation has led to misunderstanding and, in some cases, hostility between Aboriginal and non-Aboriginal Canadians on matters of importance.

It will take time and commitment to reverse this legacy. The schools operated in Canada for well over a century. In the same way, the reconciliation process will have to span generations. It will take time to re-establish respect. Effective reconciliation will see Aboriginal people regaining their sense of self-respect, and the development of relations of mutual respect between Aboriginal and non-Aboriginal people. In future reports, the Truth and Reconciliation Commission will be making specific recommendations as to how reconciliation can be furthered.

There are three points we would like to leave with all readers.

The first is that this story has heroes. The work of truth telling, healing, and reconciliation was commenced well over two decades ago by the people who, as children, had been victimized by this system. They continue to do the heavy labour of sharing their stories, and, by so doing, educating their children, their communities, and their country.

The second is obvious: a commission such as this cannot itself achieve reconciliation. Reconciliation implies relationship. The residential schools badly damaged relationships within Aboriginal families and communities, between Aboriginal peoples and churches, between Aboriginal peoples and the government, and between

Aboriginal and non-Aboriginal peoples within Canadian society. The Commissioners believe these relationships can and must be repaired. The Indian Residential Schools Settlement Agreement is a positive step in this process since it formally recognized the need to come to terms with the past. The process of reconciliation will require the passionate commitment of individuals and the genuine engagement of society. There are people today who are living with the direct impacts of the schools: the survivors and their families. Specific attention will have to be paid to their needs. The conflicts that have arisen within communities as a result of the school system must be recognized and addressed. Churches have to define their role in this process as Aboriginal people reclaim what is of value to them.

Reconciliation also will require changes in the relationship between Aboriginal people and the government of Canada. The federal government, along with the provincial governments, historically has taken a social welfare approach to its dealings with Aboriginal people. This approach fails to recognize the unique legal status of Aboriginal peoples as the original peoples of this country. Without that recognition, we run the risk of continuing the assimilationist policies and the social harms that were integral to the residential schools.

Finally, there is no reason for anyone who wants to contribute to the reconciliation process to wait until the publication of the Commission's final reports. There is an opportunity now for Canadians to engage in this work, to make their own contributions to reconciliation, and to create new truths about our country. As Assembly of First Nations National Chief Phil Fontaine observed when he accepted Canada's apology in June 2008, "Together we can achieve the greatness our country deserves." Our challenge and opportunity will be to work together to achieve that greatness.

Appendix A

The Mandate of the Truth and Reconciliation Commission

Schedule N of the Indian Residential Schools Settlement Agreement

There is an emerging and compelling desire to put the events of the past behind us so that we can work towards a stronger and healthier future. The truth telling and reconciliation process as part of an overall holistic and comprehensive response to the Indian Residential School legacy is a sincere indication and acknowledgement of the injustices and harms experienced by Aboriginal people and the need for continued healing. This is a profound commitment to establishing new relationships embedded in mutual recognition and respect that will forge a brighter future. The truth of our common experiences will help set our spirits free and pave the way to reconciliation.

Principles

Through the Agreement, the Parties have agreed that an historic Truth and Reconciliation Commission will be established to contribute to truth, healing and reconciliation.

The Truth and Reconciliation Commission will build upon the "Statement of Reconciliation" dated January 7, 1998 and the principles developed by the Working Group on Truth and Reconciliation and of the Exploratory Dialogues (1998-1999). These principles are as follows: accessible; victim-centered; confidentiality (if required by the former student); do no harm; health and safety of participants; representative; public/transparent; accountable; open and honourable process; comprehensive; inclusive, educational, holistic, just and fair; respectful; voluntary; flexible; and forward looking in terms of rebuilding and renewing Aboriginal relationships and the relationship between Aboriginal and non-Aboriginal Canadians.

Reconciliation is an ongoing individual and collective process, and will require commitment from all those affected including First Nations, Inuit and Métis former Indian Residential School (IRS) students, their families, communities, religious entities, former school employees, government and the people of Canada. Reconciliation may occur between any of the above groups.

Terms of Reference

1. Goals

The goals of the Commission shall be to:

(a) Acknowledge Residential School experiences, impacts and consequences;

(b) Provide a holistic, culturally appropriate and safe setting for former students, their families and communities as they come forward to the Commission;

(c) Witness[1], support, promote and facilitate truth and reconciliation events at both the national and community levels;

(d) Promote awareness and public education of Canadians about the IRS system and its impacts;

(e) Identify sources and create as complete an historical record as possible of the IRS system and legacy. The record shall be preserved and made accessible to the public for future study and use;

(f) Produce and submit to the Parties of the Agreement[2] a report including recommendations[3] to the Government of Canada concerning the IRS system and experience including: the history, purpose, operation and supervision of the IRS system, the effect and consequences of IRS (including systemic harms, intergenerational consequences and the impact on human dignity) and the ongoing legacy of the residential schools;

---

1 This refers to the Aboriginal principle of "witnessing."

2 The Government of Canada undertakes to provide for wider dissemination of the report pursuant to the recommendations of the Commissioners.

3 The Commission may make recommendations for such further measures as it considers necessary for the fulfillment of the Truth and Reconciliation Mandate and goals.

(g) Support commemoration of former Indian Residential School students and their families in accordance with the Commemoration Policy Directive (Schedule "X" of the Agreement).

2. Establishment, Powers, Duties and Procedures of the Commission

The Truth and Reconciliation Commission shall be established by the appointment of "the Commissioners" by the Federal Government through an Order in Council, pursuant to special appointment regulations.

Pursuant to the Court-approved final settlement agreement and the class action judgments, the Commissioners:

(a) in fulfilling their Truth and Reconciliation Mandate, are authorized to receive statements and documents from former students, their families, community and all other interested participants, and, subject to (f), (g) and (h) below, make use of all documents and materials produced by the parties. Further, the Commissioners are authorized and required in the public interest to archive all such documents, materials, and transcripts or recordings of statements received, in a manner that will ensure their preservation and accessibility to the public and in accordance with access and privacy legislation, and any other applicable legislation;

(b) shall not hold formal hearings, nor act as a public inquiry, nor conduct a formal legal process;

(c) shall not possess subpoena powers, and do not have powers to compel attendance or participation in any of its activities or events. Participation in all Commission events and activities is entirely voluntary;

(d) may adopt any informal procedures or methods they may consider expedient for the proper conduct of the Commission events and activities, so long as they remain consistent with the goals and provisions set out in the Commission's mandate statement;

(e) may, at its discretion, hold sessions in camera, or require that sessions be held in camera;

(f) shall perform their duties in holding events, in activities, in public meetings, in consultations, in making public statements, and in making their report and recommendations without making any findings or expressing any conclusion or recommendation, regarding the misconduct of any person, unless such findings or information has already been established through legal proceedings, by admission, or by public disclosure by the individual. Further, the Commission shall not make any reference in any of its activities or in its report or recommendations to the possible civil or criminal liability of any person or organization, unless such findings or information about the individual or institution has already been established through legal proceedings;

(g) shall not, except as required by law, use or permit access to statements made by individuals during any of the Commissions events, activities or processes, except with the express consent of the individual and only for the sole purpose and extent for which the consent is granted;

(h) shall not name names in their events, activities, public statements, report or recommendations, or make use of personal information or of statements made which identify a person, without the express consent of that individual, unless that information and/or the identity of the person so identified has already been established through legal proceedings, by admission, or by public disclosure by that individual. Other information that could be used to identify individuals shall be anonymized to the extent possible;

(i) notwithstanding (e), shall require in camera proceedings for the taking of any statement that contains names or other identifying information of persons alleged by the person making the statement of some wrong doing, unless the person named or identified has been convicted for the alleged wrong doing. The Commissioners shall not record the names of persons so identified, unless the person named or identified has been convicted for the alleged wrong doing. Other information that could be used to identify said individuals shall be anonymized to the extent possible;

(j) shall not, except as required by law, provide to any other proceeding, or for any other use, any personal information, statement made by the individual or any information identifying any person, without that individual's express consent;

(k) shall ensure that the conduct of the Commission and its activities do not jeopardize any legal proceeding;

(l) may refer to the NAC for determination of disputes involving document production, document disposal and archiving, contents of the Commission's Report and Recommendations and Commission decisions regarding the scope of its research and issues to be examined. The Commission shall make best efforts to resolve the matter itself before referring it to the NAC.

3. Responsibilities

In keeping with the powers and duties of the Commission, as enumerated in section 2 above, the Commission shall have the following responsibilities:

(a) to employ interdisciplinary, social sciences, historical, oral traditional and archival methodologies for statement-taking, historical fact-finding and analysis, report-writing, knowledge management and archiving;

(b) to adopt methods and procedures which it deems necessary to achieve its goals;

(c) to engage the services of such persons including experts, which it deems necessary to achieve its goals;

(d) to establish a research centre and ensure the preservation of its archives;

(e) to have available the use of such facilities and equipment as is required, within the limits of appropriate guidelines and rules;

(f) to hold such events and give such notices as appropriate. This shall include such significant ceremonies as the Commission sees fit during and at the conclusion of the 5 year process;

(g) to prepare a report;

(h) to have the report translated in the two official languages of Canada and all or parts of the report in such Aboriginal languages as determined by the Commissioners;

(i) to evaluate commemoration proposals in line with the Commemoration Policy Directive (Schedule "J" of the Agreement).

4. Exercise of Duties

As the Commission is not to act as a public inquiry or to conduct a formal legal process, it will, therefore, not duplicate in whole or in part the function of criminal investigations, the Independent Assessment Process, court actions, or make recommendations on matters already covered in the Agreement. In the exercise of its powers the Commission shall recognize:

(a) the unique experiences of First Nations, Inuit and Métis former IRS students, and will conduct its activities, hold its events, and prepare its Report and Recommendations in a manner that reflects and recognizes The unique experiences of all former IRS students;

(b) that the truth and reconciliation process is committed to the principle of voluntariness with respect to individuals' participation;

(c) that it will build upon the work of past and existing processes, archival records, resources and documentation, including the work and records of the Royal Commission on Aboriginal Peoples of 1996;

(d) the significance of Aboriginal oral and legal traditions in its activities;

(e) that as part of the overall holistic approach to reconciliation and healing, the Commission should reasonably coordinate with other initiatives under the Agreement and shall acknowledge links to other aspects of the Agreement such that the overall goals of reconciliation will be promoted;

(f) that all individual statements are of equal importance, even if these statements are delivered after the completion of the report;

(g) that there shall be an emphasis on both information collection/storage and information analysis.

5. Membership

The Commission shall consist of an appointed Chairperson and two Commissioners, who shall be persons of recognized integrity, stature and respect.

(a) Consideration should be given to at least one of the three members being an Aboriginal person;

(b) Appointments shall be made out of a pool of candidates nominated by former students, Aboriginal organizations, churches and government;

(c) The Assembly of First Nations (AFN) shall be consulted in making the final decision as to the appointment of the Commissioners.

6. Secretariat

The Commission shall operate through a central Secretariat.

(a) There shall be an Executive Director in charge of the operation of the Commission who shall select and engage staff and regional liaisons;

(b) The Executive Director and the Secretariat shall be subject to the direction and control of the Commissioners;

(c) The Secretariat shall be responsible for the activities of the Commission such as:

    (i) research;

    (ii) event organization;

    (iii) statement taking/truth-sharing;

    (iv) obtaining documents;

    (v) information management of the Commission's documents;

    (vi) production of the report;

    (vii) ensuring the preservation of its records;

    (viii) evaluation of the Commemoration Policy Directive proposals.

(d) The Executive Director and Commissioners shall consult with the Indian Residential School Survivor Committee on the appointment of the Regional Liaisons.

(e) Regional liaisons shall:

    (i) act as knowledge conduits and promote sharing of knowledge among communities, individuals and the Commission;

    (ii) provide a link between the national body and communities for the purpose of coordinating national and community events;

    (iii) provide information to and assist communities as they plan truth and reconciliation events, coordinate statement-taking/truth-sharing and event-recording, and facilitate information flow from the communities to the Commission.

7. Indian Residential School Survivor Committee (IRSSC)

The Commission shall be assisted by an Indian Residential School Survivor Committee (IRSSC).

(a) The Committee shall be composed of 10 representatives drawn from various Aboriginal organizations and survivor groups. Representation shall be regional, reflecting the population distribution of Indian Residential Schools (as defined in the Agreement). The majority of the representatives shall be former residential school students;

(b) Members of the Committee shall be selected by the Federal Government, in consultation with the AFN, from a pool of eligible candidates developed by the stakeholders;

(c) Committee members are responsible for providing advice to the Commissioners on:

    (i) the characteristics of a "community" for the purposes of participation in the Commission processes;

    (ii) the criteria for the community and national processes;

    (iii) the evaluation of Commemoration Policy Directive proposals;

    (iv) such other issues as are required by the Commissioners.

8. Timeframe

The Commission shall complete its work within five years. Within that five year span, there are two timelines:

Two Year Timeline

(a) Preparation of a budget within three months from being launched, under the budgetary cap provision in the Agreement;

(b) Completion of all national events, and research and production of the report on historic findings and recommendations, within two years of the launch of the Commission, with the possibility of a 6 month extension, which shall be at the discretion of the Commissioners.

Five Year Timeline

(a) Completion of the community truth and reconciliation events, statement taking/truth sharing, reporting to the Commission from communities, and closing ceremonies;

(b) Establishment of a research centre.

9. Research

The Commission shall conduct such research, receive and take such statements and consider such documents as it deems necessary for the purpose of achieving its goals.

10. Events

There are three essential event components to the Truth and Reconciliation Commission: National Events, Community Events and Individual Statement-Taking/Truth Sharing. The Truth and Reconciliation process will be concluded with a final Closing Ceremony.

(A) National Events

The national events are a mechanism through which the truth and reconciliation process will engage the Canadian public and provide education about the IRS system, the experience of former students and their families, and the ongoing legacies of the institutions.

The Commission shall fund and host seven national events in different regions across the country for the purpose of:

    (a) sharing information with/from the communities;

    (b) supporting and facilitating the self empowerment of former IRS students and those affected by the IRS legacy;

    (c) providing a context and meaning for the Common Experience Payment;

    (d) engaging and educating the public through mass communications;

    (e) otherwise achieving its goals.

The Commission shall, in designing the events, include in its consideration the history and demographics of the IRS system.

National events should include the following common components:

    (f) an opportunity for a sample number of former students and families to share their experiences;

    (g) an opportunity for some communities in the regions to share their experiences as they relate to the impacts on communities and to share insights from their community reconciliation processes;

    (h) an opportunity for participation and sharing of information and knowledge among former students, their families, communities, experts, church and government officials, institutions and the Canadian public;

    (i) ceremonial transfer of knowledge through the passing of individual statement transcripts or community reports/statements. The Commission shall recognize that ownership over IRS experiences rests with those affected by the Indian Residential School legacy;

    (j) analysis of the short and long term legacy of the IRS system on individuals, communities, groups, institutions and Canadian society including the intergenerational impacts of the IRS system;

    (k) participation of high level government and church officials;

    (l) health supports and trauma experts during and after the ceremony for all participants.

(B) Community Events

It is intended that the community events will be designed by communities and respond to the needs of the former students, their families and those affected by the IRS legacy including the special needs of those communities where Indian Residential Schools were located.

The community events are for the purpose of:

    (a) acknowledging the capacity of communities to develop reconciliation practices;

    (b) developing collective community narratives about the impact of the IRS system on former students, families and communities;

    (c) involving church, former school employees and government officials in the reconciliation process, if requested by communities;

    (d) creating a record or statement of community narratives – including truths, insights and recommendations–for use in the historical research and report, national events, and for inclusion in the research centre;

    (e) educating the public and fostering better relationships with local communities;

    (f) allowing for the participation from high level government and church officials, if requested by communities;

    (g) respecting the goal of witnessing in accordance with Aboriginal principles.

The Commission, during the first stages of the process in consultation with the IRSSC, shall develop the core criteria and values consistent with the Commission's mandate that will guide the community processes.

Within these parameters communities may submit plans for reconciliation processes to the Commission and receive funding for the processes within the limits of the Commission's budgetary capacity.

(C) Individual Statement-Taking/Truth Sharing

The Commission shall coordinate the collection of individual statements by written, electronic or other appropriate means. Notwithstanding the five year mandate, anyone affected by the IRS legacy will be permitted to file a personal statement in the research centre with no time limitation.

The Commission shall provide a safe, supportive and sensitive environment for individual statement-taking/truth sharing.

The Commission shall not use or permit access to an individual's statement made in any Commission processes, except with the express consent of the individual.

(D) Closing Ceremony

The Commission shall hold a closing ceremony at the end of its mandate to recognize the significance of all events over the life of the Commission. The closing ceremony shall have the participation of high level church and government officials.

11. Access to Relevant Information

In order to ensure the efficacy of the truth and reconciliation process, Canada and the churches will provide all relevant documents in their possession or control to and for the use of the Truth and Reconciliation Commission, subject to the privacy interests of an individual as provided by applicable privacy legislation, and subject to and in compliance with applicable privacy and access to information legislation, and except for those documents for which solicitor-client privilege applies and is asserted.

In cases where privacy interests of an individual exist, and subject to and in compliance with applicable privacy legislation and access to information legislation, researchers for the Commission shall have access to the documents, provided privacy is protected. In cases where solicitor-client privilege is asserted, the asserting party will provide a list of all documents for which the privilege is claimed.

Canada and the churches are not required to give up possession of their original documents to the Commission. They are required to compile all relevant documents in an organized manner for review by the Commission and to provide access to their archives for the Commission to carry out its mandate. Provision of documents does not require provision of original documents. Originals or true copies may be provided or originals may be provided temporarily for copying purposes if the original documents are not to be housed with the Commission.

Insofar as agreed to by the individuals affected and as permitted by process requirements, information from the Independent Assessment Process (IAP), existing litigation and Dispute Resolution processes may be transferred to the Commission for research and archiving purposes.

12. National Research Centre

A research centre shall be established, in a manner and to the extent that the Commission's budget makes possible. It shall be accessible to former students, their families and communities, the general public, researchers and educators who wish to include this historic material in curricula.

For the duration of the term of its mandate, the Commission shall ensure that all materials created or received pursuant to this mandate shall be preserved and archived with a purpose and tradition in keeping with the objectives and spirit of the Commission's work.

The Commission shall use such methods and engage in such partnerships with experts, such as Library and Archives Canada, as are necessary to preserve and maintain the materials and documents. To the extent feasible and taking into account the relevant law and any recommendations by the Commission concerning the continued confidentiality of records, all materials collected through this process should be accessible to the public.

13. Privacy

The Commission shall respect privacy laws, and the confidentiality concerns of participants. For greater certainty:

(a) any involvement in public events shall be voluntary;

(b) notwithstanding 2(i), the national events shall be public or in special circumstances, at the discretion of the Commissioners, information may be taken in camera;

(c) the community events shall be private or public, depending upon the design provided by the community;

(d) if an individual requests that a statement be taken privately, the Commission shall accommodate;

(e) documents shall be archived in accordance with legislation.

14. Budget and Resources

The Commission shall prepare a budget within the first three months of its mandate and submit it to the Minister of Indian Residential Schools Resolution Canada for approval. Upon approval of its budget, it will have full authority to make decisions on spending, within the limits of, and in accordance with, its Mandate, its establishing Order in Council, Treasury Board policies, available funds, and its budgetary capacity.

The Commission shall ensure that there are sufficient resources allocated to the community events over the five year period. The Commission shall also ensure that a portion of the budget is set aside for individual statement-taking/truth sharing and to archive the Commission's records and information.

Institutional parties shall bear the cost of participation and attendance in Commission events and community events, as well as provision of documents. If requested by the party providing the documents, the costs of copying, scanning, digitalizing, or otherwise reproducing the documents will be borne by the Commission.

Endnotes

CHAPTER ONE

1. Miller 1996, 103.
2. Hansard, 22 May 1883, 1377.
3. Jaenen 1986.
4. Miller 1996, 125–126.
5. Milloy 1999, 30.
6. Miller 1996, 125; Tobias 1991, 221–223.
7. Miller 2009, 156.
8. Carter 1999, 113; Friesen 1999, 207–212; Tobias 1991, 213–225.
9. Miller 2009, 156.
10. Carter 1990, 50–78; Friesen 1999, 207–212; Taylor 1999, 5–6; Tobias 1991, 211–232.
11. McMillan and Yellowhorn 2004; Fear-Segal 2007, xx.
12. McMillan and Yellowhorn 2004, 23, 152; Barman, Hébert, and McCaskill 1986, 2.
13. McMillan and Yellowhorn 2004, 118, 152.
14. McMillan and Yellowhorn 2004, 58–62, 153; Pettipas 1994, 43–61.
15. McMillan and Yellowhorn 2004, 56–62, 278.
16. McMillan and Yellowhorn 2004, 112–114.
17. Cruikshank 1991, 73.
18. Canadien 2010, 25.
19. Knockwood 2001, 17.
20. Moran 1997, 35–36.
21. French 1976, 60–61.
22. Dickson 1993, 32.
23. McMillan and Yellowhorn 2004, 82, 112–114; Smith 1987, 15.
24. Miller 1996, 44.
25. Barman, Hébert, and McCaskill 1986, 3; Jaenen 1973, 88.
26. Brody 1987, 141.
27. MacLean 2005, 107.
28. Miller 1996, 85.
29. Shingwauk 1872, 14.
30. Morris 1880, 96.
31. Henderson 1995, 247–249.
32. Morris 1880, 292.
33. Adams 1995; Fear-Segal 2007.
34. Davin 1879, 5-7.
35. Davin 1879, 9.
36. Davin 1879, 11.
37. Davin 1879, 11.
38. Davin 1879, 10.
39. Davin 1879, 10.
40. Davin 1879, 14.
41. Davin 1879, 15.
42. Indian and Northern Affairs Canada, File 1/25-1 Volume 15, L. Vankoughnet to Sir John A. Macdonald, 26 August 1887, quoted in Milloy 1999, 26.
43. Library and Archives Canada, RG 10, Volume 6039, File 160—1 MR 8152. November 1912, the Archbishop of St. Boniface to Sir Richard Rogers, quoted in Milloy 1999, 27.
44. *An Act for the Gradual Enfranchisement of Indians, the Better Management of Indian Affairs, and to Extend the Provisions of the Act*, 31st Victoria, Chapter 42, Statutes of Canada 1869.
45. Milloy 1983, 61.
46. Library and Archives Canada, RG 10, Volume 6810, File 470-2-3, volume 7, Evidence of D.C. Scott to the Special Committee of the House of Commons Investigating the *Indian Act* amendments of 1920, 63 (N-3), quoted in Moore, Leslie, and Maguire 1978, 114.
47. Report of the Department of Indian Affairs for the Year ended 31 December 1889, 165, quoted in Titley 1993, 119–120.
48. Department of Indian Affairs, Annual Report 1897, *Canada, Sessional Papers (14) 1898*, xxvii, quoted in Miller 1996, 158.
49. *Debates* 1897, column 4076, 14 June 1897, quoted in Hall 1977, 134.
50. Library and Archives Canada, RG 85, Volume 1507, File 600-1-1 part 7, *Report on Education in Canada's Northland*, 12 December 1954, quoted in King 1998, 66.
51. Library and Archives Canada, RG 10, Volume 3647, File 8128, MR C 10113, J.A. Macrae to Indian Commissioner, Regina, 18 December 1886, quoted in Milloy 1999, 32.
52. D.C. Scott, "Report of the Superintendent of Indian Education, 1910," in *Report of the Department of Indian Affairs* for the year ended 31 March 1910, 273.
53. Peikoff and Brickey 1991, 40.
54. Sutherland 2000, 107.
55. Huel 1996, 119–120.

56. Bullen 1991, 139–140.
57. Choquette 1995; Huel 1996; Usher 1974.
58. Choquette 1995, 1–20.
59. Choquette 2004, 192–194.
60. Stevenson 1988, 133–136.
61. Moorhouse 1973, 274.
62. Henry Venn, to James Quaker, 29 November 1853, cited in W. Knight, *The Missionary Secretariat of Henry Venn, B.D.* (London: Longmans, Green, 1880, p. 53), quoted in Usher 1974, 22.
63. Hare and Barman 2006; McPherson 1995; Rutherdale 2002.
64. Huel 1996, 69–71.
65. Morantz 2002, 213.
66. Choquette 2004, 56.
67. William Duncan, Journal number 2 1857, reel 2154, William Duncan Papers, Special Collections, University of British Columbia, quoted in Higham 2000, 56.
68. Pettipas 1994, 87–125.
69. LaViolette 1961, 41.
70. Grant 1985, 242.
71. Miller 1996, 126.
72. Miller 1996, 157.
73. Milloy 1999, 72.
74. Milloy 1999, 77.
75. General Synod Archives, Anglican Church of Canada, M75-103 series 2-14, Missionary Society of the Church in Canada, Frank Oliver to the Anglican Church of Canada, 28 January 1908, in Coates 1991, 146.
76. Grant 1985, 192–195.
77. Miller 1996, 141.
78. Milloy 1999, 94–95.
79. Milloy 1999, 70–71.
80. Coccola 1988, 175.
81. Johnston 1988, 19–20.
82. Persson 1986, 157.
83. Kelm 2003, 98.
84. Whitehead 1988, 62.
85. Goodwill and Sluman 1984, 190.
86. Miller 1996, 142.
87. Miller 1996, 313.
88. Milloy 1999, 102.
89. Milloy 1999, 103–105.
90. Milloy 1999, 332.
91. Barman, Hébert, and McCaskill 1986, 9.
92. Miller 1996, 390.
93. Milloy 1999, 176.
94. Miller 1996, 389.
95. Hawthorn 1967, 88.
96. Milloy 1999, 226.
97. Miller 1996, 393.
98. Milloy 1999, 227.
99. Milloy 1996, 214.
100. Milloy 1996, 214.
101. Indian and Northern Affairs Canada, File 40-2-185, Volume 1, *Relationships between Church and State in Indian Education*, 26 September 1966, quoted in Milloy 1999, 214.
102. Johnston 1983, 57.
103. Milloy 1999, 215.
104. Canadian Welfare Council 1967, 151.
105. Persson 1986, 164–167.
106. Dyck 1997, 120.

CHAPTER TWO

1. Peequaquat 1991, 69.
2. Baker 1994, 28.
3. Dickson 1993, 119.
4. Willis 1973, 136.
5. Knockwood 2001, 27.
6. Thrasher 1976, 3–4.
7. Mountain Horse 1979, 15.
8. Blondin-Perrin 2009, 12–13.
9. Mountain Horse 1979, 15.
10. Janvier 2004, 19.
11. Callahan 2002, 39–40.
12. Brass 1987, 22.
13. Elias 2010, 52.
14. Stevenson 1988, 137.
15. French 1976, 19.
16. Ford 1971, 93–94.
17. Willis 1973, 31–32.
18. Gresko 1992, 80.
19. Blondin-Perrin 2009, 17.
20. Marguerite 2010, 57.
21. Dickson 1993, 120.
22. French 1976, 20.
23. Anonymous, Jack, ed. 2006, 198.
24. Blondin-Perrin 2009, 38.
25. Deiter 1999, 56.
26. Driben and Trudeau 1983, 25.
27. Joe 1996, 50–51.
28. Johnston 1988, 138.
29. Provincial Archives of Alberta, Oblates of Mary Immaculate, école Dunbow, Boîte 80, #3381, *Journal quotidien de l'école Dunbow*, 8 August 1888, quoted in Pettit 1997, 265.
30. Charland 1995, 29.
31. Campbell 1973, 44.
32. Speare 1973, 19.
33. Callahan 2002, 78.
34. Library and Archives Canada, RG 10, Volume 6455, File 885-1, part 2, Edward Elliot to D.C. Scott, Deputy Superintendent General of Indian Affairs, 20 October 1919, quoted in Pettit 1997, 306.
35. Sandy 2006, 133.
36. Schmalz 1991, 187; Willis 1973, 186.
37. Department of Indian Affairs, *Annual Report* 1896, 398–399, quoted in Milloy 1999, 38.
38. Speare 1973, 7.
39. Knockwood 2001, 98.
40. Harry 2010, 37
41. Moran 1997, 60–61.
42. Library and Archives Canada, RG 10, File 57799, H. Reed to L. Vankoughnet, 14 May 1889, quoted in Gresko 1992, 88.
43. *Debates*, 1904, columns 6946–1656, 18 July 1904, quoted in Hall 1977, 134.
44. Library and Archives Canada, RG 10 Volume 4042, File 336877, 4-7, H.B. Bury, 7 November 1917, "Report on Indian Affairs – Education" (manuscript), quoted in Carney 1981, 69.
45. Barman, Hébert, and McCaskill, 1986, 9; Jamplosky 1965, 54.
46. Jamplosky 1965, 49.
47. Gooderham 1965, 100.
48. Fiske 1989, 261–262.
49. Bird 1991, 13.
50. Knockwood 2001, 53–54.
51. Arnouse 2006, 129.
52. Ron Ignace 2006, 7.
53. Raibmon 1996, 82–83.
54. Library and Archives Canada, RG 10, Volume 7185, File 1/25-1-7-1, R.T. Ferrier to C.E. Silcox, 7 April 1932, quoted in Milloy 1999, 178.
55. Acoose 1995, 5.
56. Funk 1995, 65.
57. Duncan 2006, 56.
58. Department of Indian Affairs Annual Report, 1912, 399, quoted in Barman 2003, 63.
59. Titley, *A Narrow Vision*, 1986, 90.
60. Graham 1997, 15.
61. Dyck 1997, 100–104.
62. Hildebrand 2003, 167.

63. King 1967, 56.
64. Callahan 2002, 74.
65. Lux 2001, 107.
66. Titley, "Dunbow Indian Industrial School," 1992, 105.
67. Provincial Archives of Alberta, Oblates of Mary Immaculate, école Dunbow, Boîte 80, #3381, *Journal quotidien de l'école Dunbow*, 18 January 1916, quoted in Pettit 1997, 254.
68. Titley, "Red Deer Industrial School," 1992, 59.
69. Waldram, Herring, and Young 2006, 48–49, 68–70.
70. Bryce 1907, 18.
71. Bryce 1907, 18.
72. Milloy 1999, 92.
73. Kelm 2003, 90–91.
74. Milloy 1999, 329.
75. Lux 2001, 131.
76. Titley, *A Narrow Vision*, 1986, 85.
77. Milloy 1999, 94.
78. Scott 1913, 615.
79. Titley, *A Narrow Vision*, 1986, 87.
80. Titley, *A Narrow Vision*, 1986, 57.
81. Library and Archives Canada, RG 10, Volume 3921, File 116, 818-1B, J.F. Woodsworth to Department Secretary, 25 November 1918, quoted in Titley, "Red Deer Industrial School," 1992, 65.
82. Milloy 1999, 97.
83. Titley, "Dunbow Indian Industrial School," 1992, 111.
84. Kelm 2003, 92.
85. Milloy 1999, 77.
86. Ford 1971, 102–103.
87. Ahenakew 1973, 132.
88. Brass 1987, 31.
89. George 2003, 28.
90. Willis 1973, 77.
91. King 1998, 97.
92. Waldram, Herring, and Young 2006, 188–198; Wherritt 1977, 109–110.
93. Library and Archives Canada, Canadian Tuberculosis Association, quoted in Wherritt 1977, 111.
94. Wherritt 1977, 110.
95. Milloy 1999, 89–99.
96. Smith 1996, 344.
97. Manuel and Posluns 1974, 65.
98. James 1995, 104.
99. Callahan 2002, 109.

100. Shaw 2004, 7.
101. Meltenberger 2004, 27.
102. Anonymous, Métis Nation, ed. 2004, 61.
103. Schroeder 2006, 37.
104. Moran 1997, 53.
105. Thrasher 1976, 14, 28.
106. Irniq 2010, 100–101.
107. Fontaine 1995, 51.
108. Baker 1994, 30; Milloy 1999, 114.
109. Milloy 1999, 120.
110. Brass 1987, 25–26.
111. French 1976, 44.
112. Manuel and Posluns 1974, 66.
113. Manuel and Posluns 1974, 65.
114. Collison 1995, 36.
115. Knockwood 2001, 80.
116. Manuel and Posluns 1974, 66.
117. Brass 1987, 24.
118. Brewer 2006, 27.
119. Sandy 2006, 134.
120. Sheni7 2006, 125.
121. French 1976, 52.
122. Milloy 1999, 117.
123. PeeAce 1991, 68.
124. Anonymous, Métis Nation, ed. 2004, 15.
125. Johnston 1988, 139–143.
126. Sworn information of Ellen Charlie, 28 February 1902, Alkali Lake, quoted in Furniss 1995, 67.
127. Sworn information of Christine Haines, 28 February 1902, Alkali Lake, quoted in Furniss 1995, 67.
128. Sworn information of Johnny Sticks, 28 February 1902, Alkali Lake, quoted in Furniss 1995, 69.
129. Milloy 1999, 263–265.
130. Milloy 1999, 121.
131. Milloy 1999, 265.
132. Library and Archives Canada, RG 10, Volume 3918, File 116659-1, MR C 10161, J. Smith to Assistant Deputy and Secretary, 8 February 1918, quoted in Milloy 1999, 113.
133. Library and Archives Canada, RG 10, Volume 6033, File 150-44 (2), MR C 8149, Report of Food Survey and Spanish School, 11–15 March 1945, quoted in Milloy 1999, 264.
134. Library and Archives Canada RG 10, Volume 6033, File 150-44 (2), MR C 8149, Mrs. A. Stevenson, Red Cross Survey, St. John's, Chapleau, October 1944, quoted in Milloy 1999, 264.

135. Library and Archives Canada, RG 10, Volume 6033, File 150-44 (2), MR C 8149, R. Hoey to Mrs. A. Stevenson, 15 September 1945, Mrs. A. Stevenson to R. Hoey from Mrs. A Stevenson, 8 March 1946, quoted in Milloy 1999, 263.
136. Milloy 1999, 369.
137. Gregoire 2006, 141.
138. Blondin-Perrin 2009, 134.
139. Jules 2006, 65.
140. Library and Archives Canada, RG 10 Volume 3930, File 117377-1A MR C 10163, H. Reed to Bishop of Rupert's Land, 31 May 1893, quoted in Milloy 1999, 120.
141. Library and Archives Canada, RG 10, Volume 6039, File 160-1, MR C 8152, M. Benson to J.D. McLean, 15 July 1897, quoted in Milloy 1999, 120.
142. Library and Archives Canada, RG 10, Volume 3933, File 117657-1A, M. Benson to D.C. Scott, 12 January 1918, quoted in Milloy 1999, 169.
143. Pettit 1997, 72.
144. Pettit 1997, 185.
145. Milloy 1999, 171.
146. Library and Archives Canada, RG 10 Volume 8452, File 773/23-5-003, MR C 14234, W. Graham to Secretary, 9 June 1930, quoted in Milloy 1999, 169.
147. Manuel and Posluns 1974, 64.
148. Thommasen 1993, 22.
149. Strapp to Phelan, 19 September 1945, in Graham 1997, 338.
150. Milloy 1999, 163.
151. Fiske 1996, 172–173.
152. Fiske 1996, 172.
153. Joe 1996, 52.
154. Thomson-Millward 1997, 117–118.
155. Funk 1995, 67.
156. Ledoux 1991, 61.
157. Johnston 1991, 55.
158. Titley, "Dunbow Indian Industrial School," 1992, 100.
159. Milloy 1999, 45.
160. Library and Archives Canada, RG 10, Volume 6452, File 884-1 (1-3), MR C 8773-8774, L. Vankoughnet to Bishop of Westminster, 17 October 1889, quoted in Milloy 1999, 45.
161. Milloy 1999, 45.

162. Axelrod 1997, 59–60.
163. Sutherland 2000, 138.
164. Pettit 1997, 262.
165. Pettit 1997, 262.
166. Library and Archives Canada, RG 10, Volume 3920 File 116818, MR C 10161, D.L. Clink to Indian Commissioner, 4 June 1896, quoted in Milloy 1999, 141.
167. Pettit 1997, 262.
168. Milloy 1999, 139.
169. Milloy 1999, 138.
170. Gladstone 1967, 22–23.
171. Knockwood 2001, 148–156.
172. "Jury Hears How 4 Indian Boys Froze to Death," *Winnipeg Tribune*, 5 January 1937; "Visits [to] Indian Schools. R.A. Hoey, Ottawa Official on Inspection Trip," *Montreal Gazette*, 7 January 1937; "Indian Boys' Death Subject of Inquiry," Ottawa *Journal*, 5 January 1937, quoted in Kelm 2003, 99.
173. Milloy 1999, 144.
174. Milloy 1999, 110.
175. Milloy 1999, 340.
176. Knockwood 2001, 45.
177. Dickson 1993, 84.
178. Milloy 1999, 139–140.
179. Ruben 2010, 129.
180. James 1995, 104.
181. Jules 2006, 61.
182. Anonymous, Métis Nation, ed. 2004, 121.
183. Willis 1973, 34–35.
184. Marchand 2006, 30.
185. Knockwood 2001, 97.
186. Bush 2000, 110.
187. Milloy 1999, 339.
188. Milloy 1999, 146.
189. Library and Archives Canada, RG 10, Volume 6267, File 580-1 (1-3), MR C 8656, J. Waddy to W. Graham, 1 September 1924, quoted in Milloy 1999, 147.
190. Milloy 1999, 147.
191. Milloy 1999, 266–268.
192. Milloy 1999, 279.
193. Milloy 1999, 288.
194. Milloy 1999, 288–299; Achneepineskum 1995, 2.
195. CBC, *The Journal*, http://archives.cbc.ca/society/education/clips/11177/ (accessed 9 May 2011).

196. Indian and Northern Affairs Canada, Information Sheets – Resolution Framework, Resolution Framework to resolve Indian Residential Schools Claims, http://www.ainc-inac.gc.ca/ai/rqpi/info/nwz/2002/20021212_is-eng.asp (accessed 3 March 2011).
197. Ruben 2010, 136.
198. Choquette 1995, 158.
199. Library and Archives Canada, Hayter Reed Papers, MG 29, E 106, Volume 18, Personnel H-L, Tims to Indian Commissioner, 4 October 1891, quoted in Huel 1996, 131; Dempsey n.d.
200. Titley, "Indian Industrial Schools in Western Canada," 1986, 144.
201. In the original: "pour jouer avec les petites filles dans votre chambre, ou pour lire les magazines." Provincial Archives of Alberta, Oblates of Mary Immaculate, Dunbow, Boite 1, Correspondance 1914, H. Grandin to Père Nordmann, 4 April 1914, quoted in Titley, "Dunbow Indian Industrial School," 1992, 107.
202. Hildebrand 2003, 259.
203. United Church Central Archives, Presbyterian Church in Canada, Board of Foreign Missions, Records Pertaining to Missions to Aboriginal People in Manitoba and the North West, Box 7, File 131, P.W. Gibson Ponton to R.P. MacKay, 1 February 1911, quoted in Hildebrand 2003, 233.
204. Library and Archives Canada, RG 10, SF, Reel C7922, Volume 6187, File 461-1 part 1, Copy – "Report of Commission of Presbytery appointed to investigate conditions at Cecelia Jeffrey Boarding School," by Hugh J. Robertson and S.C. Murray, 26 February 1918, quoted in Hildebrand 2003, 235.
205. Rita Arey, statement to the Truth and Reconciliation Commission, Aklavik, Northwest Territories, 17 May 2011.
206. Anonymous, Jack, ed. 2006, 48–49.
207. Fontaine 2010, 13–19.
208. Deiter 1999, 59.
209. Mandryk 2001, 210.

210. Ethan Baron, "Residential School Abuses: 'Trauma and Loss Exposed.'" *The Province*, 16 June 2006. http://www2.canada.com/theprovince/news/story.html?id=d8c423e9-76b6-4ff5-bf4d-a291bbbb939d&p=3 (accessed 28 February 2011).
211. Shea 1999.
212. Greg Murdock, statement to the Truth and Reconciliation Commission, Winnipeg, Manitoba, 18 June 2010.
213. Baker 1994, 31.
214. Bear 1991, 43.
215. Anonymous, Jack, ed. 2006, 174.
216. Anonymous, Métis Nation, ed. 2004, 61.
217. Fontaine 1995, 51–52.
218. Amos 2006, 10.
219. Law Commission of Canada 2000, 45–46.
220. Joe 1996, 44–46.
221. Joe 1996, 49–51.
222. Joe 1996, 78.
223. Harrison 1985, 65.
224. Library and Archives Canada, RG 10, Volume 6438, note attached to Father George Forbes, Oblate of Mary Immaculate to the deputy superintendent general of Department of Indian Affairs, 7 March 1936, quoted in Coccola 1988, 62.
225. Bird 1991, 5–11, 81.
226. Mercredi 2004, 91.
227. Brewer 2006, 26; Vivian Ignace 2006, 169.
228. Amos 2006, 12.
229. Alex 2010, 10.
230. Vivian Ignace 2006, 169.
231. Gregoire 2006, 142.
232. Callahan 2002, 64.
233. Callahan 2002, 76.
234. Fontaine 2010, 96.
235. Brass 1987, 9.
236. Bear 1991, 44.
237. Willis 1973, 103–104.
238. MacGregor 1989, 24–32.
239. Irniq 2010, 111.
240. Kennedy 1972, 54; Kennedy 1970, 125; Pettipas 1994, 133.
241. Crevier n.d.
242. Morley 1967, 158.
243. Graham n.d.
244. Blondin-Andrew 2003, 64.

245. Van Camp 1989, 169.
246. Pettit 1997, 307.
247. Library and Archives Canada, RG 10, Volume 3940, File 121,698-13, O, H.R. Halpin to Indian Affairs, 28 August 1897, quoted in Ray, Miller, and Tough 2000, 194.
248. Huel 1996, 129.
249. Department of Indian Affairs, *Annual Report,* 1888, 21, quoted in Pettit 1997, 79.
250. Dyck 1997, 42.
251. Huel 1996, 129.
252. Pettit 1997, 156.
253. Brass 1987, 6.
254. Ford 1971, 90–93.
255. Cruikshank 1991, 70.
256. Tizya 1965, 103–104.
257. Library and Archives Canada, RG 10, Volume 6451, File 883-1, part 1, various correspondence, June 1922, quoted in Kelm 2003, 102.
258. James 1995, 103.
259. Brass 1987, 23–24.
260. Brownlie 2003, 133.
261. Goodwill and Sluman 1984, 196–199.
262. Pettit 1997, 310.
263. Milloy 1999, 334.
264. Pettit 1997, 69.
265. Smith n.d.
266. Cuthand 1991, 383.
267. Milloy 1999, 151–152.
268. Thomson-Millward 1997, 111.
269. Milloy 1999, 166.
270. Graham 1997, 12.
271. MacGregor 1989, 25–26.
272. Baker 1994, 36–37.
273. Bell 1995, 11–12.
274. Batten 2002, 12–13.
275. Milloy 1999, 285.
276. Furniss 1995, 62–63.
277. Milloy 1999, 285.
278. Milloy 1999, 286.
279. Milloy 1999, 286.
280. Milloy 1999, 375.
281. Milloy 1999, 286.
282. Dickson 1993, 106.
283. Roberts 2004, 52.
284. Sanderson 1991, 59.
285. Library and Archives Canada, RG 10, Volume 6320, File 658-1, part 2, 30 April 1946, J.P.B. Ostrander, Inspector of Indian Agencies, Indian Affairs Branch, Regina to Indian Affairs Branch, Ottawa, quoted in Dyck 1997, 38.
286. Titley, "Red Deer Industrial School," 1992, 60–62.
287. Blondin-Perrin 2009, 149.

CHAPTER THREE

1. Coates 1984, 179–181; Coates 1986, 132–135.
2. Yukon Territorial Archives, Anglican Church, New Series, file 2, Notes of Interview, 26 February 1909, quoted in Coates 1991, 138.
3. McCarthy 1995, 159–160; Abel 1993, 118.
4. McCarthy 1995, 164–165.
5. Crowe 1991, 166.
6. Coates 1989, 151.
7. Coates 1989, 152.
8. Coates 1989, 154; Coates 1991, 144–145.
9. Coates 1989, 159.
10. Anglican Church Records, Westgate file. Stringer to Westgate, 19 April 1923, quoted in Coates 1989, 157.
11. Coates 1989, 158.
12. Thrasher 1976, 39.
13. Mackenzie River, *The Living Message,* 12 May 1928, 149, quoted in Rutherdale 2005, 54.
14. Coates 1991, 147.
15. Cruikshank 1991, 71.
16. Coates 1989, 161; Crowe 1991, 198; McCarthy 1995, 163.
17. Coates 1991, 151.
18. King 1967, 77–78.
19. McCarthy 1995, 162.
20. Elias 2010, 54–55.
21. Abel 1993, 182.
22. Carney 1981, 68.
23. Carney 1992, 127; McCarthy 1995, 162.
24. Dickerson 1992, 41.
25. Rompkey 2003, 36–37; 46.
26. Rompkey 2003, 67.
27. Phillips 1967, 233.
28. Dickerson 1992, 39.
29. Coates 1991, 203.
30. Library and Archives Canada, RG 85, Volume 1506, File 600-1-1, Part 2A, Wright to Gibson, 19 November 1946, quoted in Duffy 1988, 96.
31. Dickerson 1992, 42–44; King 1998, 63.
32. King 1998, 63–64.
33. King 1998, 68, 78–79.
34. King 2006, 4–7.
35. Niviaxie 2010, 118–120.
36. Phillips 1967, 238.
37. Canadien 2010, 251.
38. King 2006, 7.
39. Brody 1987, 214; Coates 1991, 203; Duffy 1988, 100.
40. Duffy 1988, 99, 107.
41. King 1998, 136.
42. Phillips 1967, 240.
43. Duffy 1988, 99.
44. Library and Archives Canada RG 85, Volume 1468, File 630-125-1 part 1, E.W. Lyall to Jacobson, 25 October 1959 quoted in King 1998, 163–168.
45. Duffy 1988, 108.
46. Duffy 1988, 118.
47. Elias 2010, 51.
48. Jack Anawak, statement to the Truth and Reconciliation Commission, Iqaluit, Nunavut, 25 March 2011.
49. Wachowich 1999, 106.
50. "Education Must Fit Eskimo," *Edmonton Journal,* 22 August 1972, quoted in King 1998, 149.
51. King 1998, 86.
52. King 1998, 88–89.
53. King 1998, 92.
54. King 1998, 95–99.
55. King 1998, 105–106.
56. King 1998, 145–146.
57. Phillips 1967, 236.
58. Coates 1985, 214.
59. Hamilton 1994, 110–111.
60. Brody 1991, 210–212.
61. Peterson 1994, 5, 7, 12–13.
62. Weetaltuk 2010, 162.
63. Statistics Canada http://www.statcan.gc.ca/pub/89-519-x/2006001/c-g/4181577-eng.htm (accessed 24 March 2011).

CHAPTER FOUR

1. Davin 1879, 9.
2. Huel 1996, 100.

3. Stanley 1963, 237.
4. Erickson 2005, 17–38.
5. McMillan and Yellowhorn 2004, 300.
6. Harrison 1985, 20.
7. Carter 1999, 109–110.
8. Brody 1987, 197.
9. Chartrand 2006, 19; Daniels 2006, 117.
10. Daniels 2006, 118–119.
11. Harrison 1985, 61–65.
12. Logan 2007, 67.
13. Chartrand 2006, 41.
14. Carney 1992, 121–122.
15. McCarthy 1995, 159–160.
16. McCarthy 1995, 236.
17. McCarthy 1995, 175.
18. Gresko 1992, 79; Huel 1996, 130; Titley, "Dunbow Indian Industrial School," 1992, 99.
19. Daniels 2006, 132.
20. Huel 1996, 161.
21. Library and Archives Canada, RG 10, Volume 6031, File 150-9, part 1, C. Sifton to Smart, 13 October 1899.
22. Chartrand 2006, 44; Gresko 1992, 79.
23. Library and Archives Canada, RG 10, Volume 6031, File 150-9, part 1, W. Graham, Indian Commissioner, 17 April 1924, quoted in Logan 2006, 72.
24. Provincial Archives of Alberta, Oblates of Mary Immaculate, Paroisses noninventoriées: Brocket Correspondance 1922-29, Christianson to Le Vern, 28 August 1934, quoted in Huel 1996, 162.
25. Quiring 2004, 50–51.
26. Erickson 2005, 33.
27. Erickson 2005, 35.
28. Erickson 2011, 131.
29. Janvier, 2004, 20.
30. Stanley 1978, 90–105.
31. Anglican Church of Canada, Yukon Hostels—Dawson City and Whitehorse.
32. Daniels 2006, 125–130.
33. Chalmers 1985, 9.
34. Titley, "Dunbow Indian Industrial School," 1992, 107–108.
35. Campbell 1973, 44.
36. Dickson 1993, 86–87.
37. Larocque 2004, 36.
38. Thomas 2004, 86.
39. Crerar 2004, 126.

CHAPTER FIVE

1. Bruno-Jofre 2005, 13–14, 23–43, 77, 94–95.
2. Hildebrand 2003, 52.
3. United Church Central Archives, Presbyterian Church in Canada, Board of Foreign Missions, Records Pertaining to Missions to Aboriginal People in Manitoba and the North West, Box 2, File 4, McKitrick to Dr. Wardrop, 18 May 1891, quoted in Hildebrand 2003, 48–49.
4. Rutherdale 2002, 24–25.
5. Hildebrand 2003, 58.
6. Moore 1965, 41.
7. Hildebrand 2003, 249.
8. Hildebrand 2003, 248–250.
9. King 1967, 59.
10. Moore 1965, 40.
11. Huel 1996, 154–155.
12. Hildebrand 2003, 69.
13. Library and Archives Canada, RG 10, Volume 6446, File 882-1, part 2, Provincial Superior to D.C. Scott, 17 May 1926, quoted in Pettit 1997, 275.
14. Father Allard's Diary, quoted in Cronin 1960, 221–222.
15. Fiske 1989, 244.
16. Brass 1987, 20–21.
17. Hildebrand 2003, 103–109, 115.
18. "Hay River," *Letter Leaflet*, April 1916, 180, quoted in Rutherdale 2002, 130.
19. "Yukon," *The Living Message*, February 1928, 41, quoted in Rutherdale 2005, 54.
20. Redford 1978, 47.
21. Bush 2000, 112.
22. Pettit 1997, 149.
23. Gresko 1999, 156–163.
24. Library and Archives Canada, RG 10, Volume 393, File 117,657-1, Deputy Superintendent to the Assistant Indian Commissioner, 31 March 1894, quoted in Titley, "Dunbow Indian Industrial School," 1992, 102.
25. Pettit 1997, 274.
26. Bush 2000, 112.
27. McGovern 1994, 95.
28. McGovern 1994, 104.
29. Kennedy 1972, 54–56.
30. Brass 1987, 27; Blondin-Perrin 2009, 89.
31. CBC News. N.W.T. Priest Pochat Honoured at Funeral. 6 December 2010, http://www.cbc.ca/news/canada/north/story/2010/12/06/nwt-pochat-funeral.html (accessed 8 May 2011).
32. Irniq 2003.
33. Pettit 1997, 38.
34. Graham 1997, 14.
35. ChiefCalf 2002, 117.
36. Bush 2000, 106–107.
37. Seager to Hoey, 21 June 1945, quoted in Graham 1997, 178.
38. King 1967, 63.
39. Aariak 2011.

CHAPTER SIX

1. Dion Stout and Kipling 2003, i.
2. Ahenakew 1973, 133.
3. Goodwill and Sluman 1984, 106.
4. Grant 1985, 192–193.
5. Library and Archives Canada, RG 10, Volume 6039, File 160-1, MR C 8152, W. Graham to D.C. Scott, 23 March 1923, quoted in Milloy 1999, 157.
6. Samuel Gargan, to the Truth and Reconciliation Commission, Fort Providence, Northwest Territories, 27 April 2011.
7. Anonymous, Jack, ed. 2006, 177.
8. Bell 1995, 13.
9. Anglican Church Records, Moosehide file, Sarah-Jane Essau to Bishop, 31 August 1919, quoted in Coates 1989, 162.
10. Marius Tungilik, quoted in Legacy of Hope, ed. 2010, 149.
11. Espérance 2010, 88.
12. Pettit 1997, 304.
13. King 1967, 18.
14. Ahenakew 1973, 130-131; Greyeyes 1991, 53.
15. Janvier 2004, 23.
16. Anonymous, Jack, ed. 2006, 52.
17. Mitchell 2006, 88.
18. Amato 2004, 67.
19. Charland 1995, 31.
20. Manuel 1995, 107.

21. Bennett with Blackstock 2002, 21–23.
22. Anonymous, Jack, ed. 2006, 52.
23. Charland 1995, 31.
24. Guss 1995, 85.
25. Collison 1995, 39.
26. Weetaltuk 2010, 169.
27. Fontaine 2010, 165.
28. Sellars 1995,125.
29. Indian Residential Schools Survivor Society, "About Our Society," http://www.irsss.ca/about_us.html (accessed 23 January 2011).
30. National Residential Schools Survivors' Society, http://www.nrsss.ca (accessed 23 January 2011).
31. Hansard, June 11, 2008, 6850.
32. Hansard, June 11, 2008, 6851.
33. Hansard, June 11, 2008, 6852.
34. Hansard, June 11, 2008, 6853.
35. Hansard, June 11, 2008, 6855.
36. Hansard, June 11, 2008, 6855.
37. Hansard, June 11, 2008, 6855.
38. Hansard, June 11, 2008, 6856.
39. Hansard, June 11, 2008, 6856.

References

Aariak, Eva. "Nunavut Premier Eva Aariak Honours the Passing of Jose Kusugak." January 19, 2011. http://www.arcticcollege.ca/news/news_eng.aspx?ID=266 (accessed 27 January 2011).

Abel, Kerry. *Drum Song: Glimpses of Dene History*. Montreal and Kingston: McGill-Queen's University Press, 1993.

Achneepineskum, Pearl. "Charlie Want." In *Residential Schools: The Stolen Years*, edited by Linda Jaine. Saskatoon: University of Saskatchewan, University Extension Press, 1995.

Acoose, Janice. "Deconstructing Five Generations of White Christian Patriarchal Rule." In *Residential Schools: The Stolen Years*, edited by Linda Jaine. Saskatoon: University of Saskatchewan, University Extension Press, 1995.

Adams, David Wallace. *Education for Extinction: American Indians and the Boarding School Experience, 1875–1928*. Lawrence, KS: University Press of Kansas, 1995.

Ahenakew, Edward. *Voices of the Plains Cree*. Edited by Ruth M. Buck. Toronto: McClelland and Stewart, 1973.

Alex. "Alex." In *Collection of Life Stories of the Survivors of the Quebec Indian Residential Schools*. Edited by Richard Gray and Martine Gros-Louis Monier. Wendlake, QC: First Nations of Quebec and Labrador Health and Social Services Commission, 2010.

Amato, George. "George Amato." In *Métis Memories of Residential Schools: A Testament to the Strength of the Métis*, edited by Métis Nation of Alberta. Edmonton: Métis Nation of Alberta, 2004.

Amos, Andrew. "Andrew Amos." In *Behind Closed Doors: Stories from the Kamloops Indian Residential School*, edited by Agnes Jack. Secwepemc Cultural Education Society, Kamloops, British Columbia. Penticton: Theytus Books, 2006.

Anglican Church of Canada, Yukon Hostels — Dawson City and Whitehorse. http://www.anglican.ca/rs/history/schools/yukon-hostels.htm (accessed 22 December 2010).

Arnouse, Pauline. "Pauline Arnouse." In *Behind Closed Doors: Stories from the Kamloops Indian Residential School*, edited by Agnes Jack. Secwepemc Cultural Education Society, Kamloops, British Columbia. Penticton: Theytus Books, 2006.

Axelrod, Paul. *The Promise of Schooling: Education in Canada, 1800–1914*. Toronto: University of Toronto Press, 1997.

Baker, Simon. *Khot-La-Cha: The Autobiography of Chief Simon Baker*. Compiled and edited by Verna J. Kirkness. Vancouver: Douglas & McIntyre, 1994.

Barman, Jean. "Schooled for Inequality: The Education of British Columbia Aboriginal Children." In *Children, Teachers, & Schools: In the History of British Columbia*, edited by Jean Barman, Neil Sutherland, and J.D. Wilson. Second edition, Calgary: Detselig Enterprises, 2003.

_____, Yvonne Hébert, and Don McCaskill. "The Legacy of the Past: An Overview." In *Indian Education in Canada*. Vol. 1, *The Legacy*, edited by Jean Barman, Yvonne Hébert, and Don McCaskill. Vancouver: University of British Columbia Press, 1986.

Batten, Jack. *The Man Who Ran Faster Than Everyone: The Story of Tom Longboat*. Toronto: Tundra Books, 2002.

Bear, Shirley. "Boarding School Life." In *"… And then they told us their stories": A Book of Indian Stories*, edited by Jack Funk and Gordon Lobe. Saskatoon: Saskatoon District Tribal Council, 1991.

Bell, Rosa. "Journeys." In *Residential Schools: The Stolen Years*, edited by Linda Jaine. Saskatoon: University of Saskatchewan, University Extension Press, 1995.

Bennett, Marilyn, with Cindy Blackstock. *A Literature Review and Annotated Bibliography Focusing on Aspects of Aboriginal Child Welfare in Canada*. Ottawa: First Nations Research Site of the Centre of Excellence for Child Welfare, 2002.

Bird, Madeline, with the assistance of Sister Agnes Sutherland. *Living Kindness: The Dream of My Life*,

The Memoirs of Metis Elder, Madeline Bird. Yellowknife: Outcrop, 1991.

Blondin-Andrew, Ethel. "New Ways of Looking for Leadership." In *Leading in an Upside-Down World: New Canadian Perspectives on Leadership*, edited by J. Patrick Boyer. Toronto: Dundurn Press, 2003.

Blondin-Perrin, Alice. *My Heart Shook Like a Drum: What I Learned at the Indian Mission School, Northwest Territories.* Ottawa: Borealis Press, 2009.

Brass, Eleanor. *I Walk in Two Worlds.* Calgary: Glenbow Museum, 1987.

Brewer, William. "William Brewer." In *Behind Closed Doors: Stories from the Kamloops Indian Residential School*, edited by Agnes Jack. Secwepemc Cultural Education Society, Kamloops, British Columbia. Penticton: Theytus Books, 2006.

Brody, Hugh. *Living Arctic: Hunters of the Canadian North.* Vancouver/Toronto/Seattle: Douglas & McIntyre, 1987.

_____. *The People's Land: Inuit, Whites, and the Eastern Arctic.* Vancouver: Douglas & McIntyre, 1991.

Brownlie, Robin Jarvis. *A Fatherly Eye: Indian Agents, Government Power, and Aboriginal Resistance in Ontario, 1918–1939.* Don Mills: Oxford University Press, 2003.

Bruno-Jofre, Rosa. *The Missionary Oblate Sisters: Vision and Mission.* Montreal and Kingston: McGill-Queen's University Press, 2005.

Bryce, P.H. *Report on the Indian Schools of Manitoba and the North-West Territories.* Ottawa: Government Printing Bureau, 1907.

Bullen, John. "J.J. Kelso and the 'New' Child-Savers: The Genesis of the Children's Aid Movement in Ontario." In *Dimensions of Childhood: Essays on the History of Children and Youth in Canada*, edited by Russell Smandych, Gordon Dodds, and Alvin Esau. Winnipeg: Legal Research Institute of the University of Manitoba, 1991.

Bush, Peter. *Western Challenge: The Presbyterian Church in Canada's Mission on the Prairies and North, 1885–1925.* Winnipeg: J. Gordon Shillingford Publishing, 2000.

Callahan, Ann B. "On Our Way to Healing: Stories from the Oldest Living Generation of the File Hills Indian Residential School." Master of Arts thesis, University of Manitoba, 2002.

Campbell, Maria. *Halfbreed.* Toronto: McClelland and Stewart Limited, 1973.

Canadian Welfare Council. *Indian Residential Schools—A Research Study of Child Care Programs of Nine Residential Schools in Saskatchewan [The Caldwell Report].* G. Caldwell, Project Director. Ottawa: Canadian Welfare Council, 31 January 1967.

Canadien, Albert. *From Lishamie.* Penticton: Theytus Books, 2010.

Carney, Robert. "The Native-Wilderness Equation: Catholic and Other School Orientations in the Western Arctic." In *Canadian Catholic Historical Association: Study Sessions* 48 (1981).

_____. "Residential Schooling at Fort Chipewyan and Fort Resolution 1874–1974." In *Western Oblate Studies 2*, edited by Raymond Huel. Lewiston: The Edwin Mellon Press, 1992.

Carter, Sarah. *Aboriginal People and Colonizers of Western Canada to 1900.* Toronto: University of Toronto Press, 1999.

_____. *Lost Harvests: Prairie Indian Reserve Farmers and Government Policy.* Montreal and Kingston: McGill-Queen's University Press, 1990.

CBC News. "N.W.T. Priest Pochat Honoured at Funeral." 6 December 2010. http://www.cbc.ca/news/canada/north/story/2010/12/06/nwt-pochat-funeral.html (accessed 8 May 2011).

Chalmers, J.W. "Northland: The Founding of a Wilderness School System." *Canadian Journal of Native Education* 12, 2 (1985).

Charland, Elise. "The Courage to Change." In *Residential Schools: The Stolen Years*, edited by Linda Jaine. Saskatoon: University of Saskatchewan, University Extension Press, 1995.

Chartrand, Larry N. "Métis Residential School Participation: A Literature Review." In *Métis History and Experience and Residential Schools in Canada*, edited by Larry N. Chartrand, Tricia E. Logan, and Judy D. Daniels. Ottawa: Aboriginal Healing Foundation, 2006.

ChiefCalf, April Rosenau. "Victorian Ideologies of Gender and the Curriculum of the Regina Indian Industrial School, 1891–1910." Master of Education thesis, University of Saskatchewan, 2002.

Choquette, Robert. *Canada's Religions: An Historical Introduction.* Ottawa: University of Ottawa Press, 2004.

_____. *The Oblate Assault on Canada's Northwest.* Ottawa: University of Ottawa Press, 1995.

Coates, Kenneth. "Best Left as Indians: The Federal Government and the Indians of the Yukon, 1894–1950." *The Canadian Journal of Native Studies* 4, 2 (1984).

_____. *Best Left as Indians: Native-White Relations in the Yukon Territory, 1840–1973.* Montreal and Kingston: McGill-Queen's University Press, 1991.

_____. "'Betwixt and between': The Anglican Church and the Children of the Carcross (Choutla) Residential School, 1911–1954." In *Interpreting Canada's North: Selected Reading*, edited by Kenneth Coates and William R. Morrison. Toronto: Copp Clark Pitman Limited, 1989.

_____. *Canada's Colonies: A History of the Yukon and Northwest Territories.* Toronto: James Lorimer and Company, 1985.

_____. "A Very Imperfect Means of Education: Indian Day Schools in the Yukon Territory, 1890–1955." In *Indian Education in Canada.* Vol. 1. *The Legacy*, edited by Jean Barman, Yvonne Hébert, and Don McCaskill. Vancouver: University of British Columbia Press, 1986.

Coccola, Nicolas. *They Call Me Father: Memoirs of Father Nicolas Coccola*. Edited by Margaret Whitehead. Vancouver: University of British Columbia Press, 1988.

Collison, Art. "Healing Myself Through Our Haida Traditional Customs." In *Residential Schools: The Stolen Years*, edited by Linda Jaine. Saskatoon: University of Saskatchewan, University Extension Press, 1995.

Crerar, Angie. "Angie Crerar." In *Métis Memories of Residential Schools: A Testament to the Strength of the Métis*, edited by Métis Nation of Alberta. Edmonton: Métis Nation of Alberta, 2004.

Crevier, Charlene. "Ahenakew, Edward (1885–1961)." In *The Encyclopedia of Saskatchewan*, n.d. http://esask.uregina.ca/entry/ahenakew_edward_1885-1961.html (accessed 27 March 2011).

Cronin, Kay. *Cross in the Wilderness*. Vancouver: Mitchell Press, 1960.

Crowe, Keith. *A History of the Original People of Northern Canada*. Montreal and Kingston: McGill-Queen's University Press, 1991.

Cruikshank, Julie, in collaboration with Angela Sidney, Kitty Smith, and Annie Ned. *Life Lived Like a story: Life Stories of Three Yukon Native Elders*. Vancouver: University of British Columbia Press, 1991.

Cuthand, Stan. "The Native Peoples of the Prairie Provinces in the 1920s and 1930s." In *Sweet Promises: A Reader on Indian–White Relations in Canada*, edited by J.R. Miller. Toronto: University of Toronto Press, 1991.

Daniels, Judy D. "Ancestral Pain: Métis Memories of Residential School Project." In *Métis History and Experience and Residential Schools in Canada*, edited by Larry N. Chartrand, Tricia E. Logan, and Judy D. Daniels. Ottawa: Aboriginal Healing Foundation, 2006.

Davin, Nicholas Flood. *Report on Industrial Schools for Indians and Half-Breeds*. Ottawa, 14 March 1879.

Deiter, Constance. *From Our Mother's Arms: The Intergenerational Impact of Residential Schools in Saskatchewan*. Etobicoke: United Church Publishing House, 1999.

Dempsey, Hugh A. "Jean L'Heureux." In *Dictionary of Canadian Biography*. http://www.biographi.ca/009004-119.01-e.php?BioId=41654&query (accessed 28 February 2010).

Dickerson, Mark O. *Whose North? Political Change, Political Development, and Self-Government in the Northwest Territories*. Vancouver: University of British Columbia Press and The Arctic Institute of North America, 1992.

Dickson, Stewart. *Hey, Monias! The Story of Raphael Ironstand*. Vancouver: Arsenal Pulp Press, 1993.

Dion Stout, Madeleine, and Gregory D. Kipling. *Aboriginal People, Resilience and the Residential School Legacy*. Ottawa: The Aboriginal Healing Foundation, 2003.

Driben, Paul, and Robert S. Trudeau. *When Freedom Is Lost: The Dark Side of the Relationship between the Government and the Fort Hope Band*. Toronto: University of Toronto Press, 1983.

Duffy, R. Quinn. *The Road to Nunavut: The Progress of the Eastern Arctic Inuit since the Second World War*. Montreal and Kingston: McGill-Queen's University Press, 1988.

Duncan, Cedric. "Cedric Duncan." In *Behind Closed Doors: Stories from the Kamloops Indian Residential School*, edited by Agnes Jack. Secwepemc Cultural Education Society, Kamloops, British Columbia. Penticton: Theytus Books, 2006.

Dyck, Noel. *Differing Visions: Administering Indian Residential Schooling in Prince Albert 1867–1995*. Halifax: Fernwood Press, 1997.

Elias, Lillian. "Lillian Elias." In *We Were So Far Away: The Inuit Experience of Residential Schools*, edited by Legacy of Hope Foundation. Ottawa: Legacy of Hope, 2010.

Erickson, Lesley. "'Bury Our Sorrows in the Sacred Heart': Gender and the Métis Response to Colonialism—the Case of Sara and Louis Riel, 1848–83." In *Unsettled Pasts: Reconceiving the West through Women's History*, edited by Sarah Carter, Lesley Erickson, Patricia Roome, and Char Smith. Calgary: University of Calgary Press, 2005.

_____. "Repositioning the Missionary: Sara Riel, the Grey Nuns, and Aboriginal Women in Catholic Missions of the Northwest." In *Recollecting: Lives of Aboriginal Women of the Canadian Northwest and Borderlands*, edited by Sarah Carter and Patricia A. McCormack. Edmonton: Athabasca University Press, 2011.

Espérance. "Espérance." In *Collection of Life Stories of the Survivors of the Quebec Indian Residential Schools*, edited by Richard Gray and Martine Gros-Louis Monier. Wendlake, QC: First Nations of Quebec and Labrador Health and Social Services Commission, 2010.

Fear-Segal, Jacqueline. *White Man's Club: Schools, Race, and the Struggle of Indian Acculturation*. Lincoln and London: University of Nebraska, 2007.

Fiske, Jo-Anne. "Gender and the Paradox of Residential Education Carrier Society." In *Women of the First Nations: Power, Wisdom and Strength*, edited by Christine Miller and Patricia Chuchryk, with Marie Smallface Marule, Brenda Many Fingers, and Cheryl Deering. Winnipeg: University of Manitoba Press, 1996.

_____. "Life At Lejac." In *Sa Ts'e: Historical Perspectives on Northern British Columbia*, edited by Thomas Thorner. Prince George: College of New Caledonia Press, 1989.

Fontaine, Phil. "We Are All Born Innocent." In *Residential Schools: The Stolen Years*, edited by Linda Jaine. Saskatoon: University of Saskatchewan, University Extension Press, 1995.

Fontaine, Theodore. *Broken Circle: The Dark Legacy of Indian Residential Schools*. Vancouver: Heritage House, 2010.

Ford, Clellan S. *Smoke From Their Fires: The Life of a Kwakiutl Chief*. Hamden, CT: Archon Books, 1971.

French, Alice. *My Name Is Masak*. Winnipeg: Peguis Publishers, 1976.

Friesen, Gerald. *The Canadian Prairies: A History.* Toronto: University of Toronto Press, 1984.

Friesen, Jean. "Magnificent Gifts: The Treaties of Canada with the Indians of the Northwest 1869–1876." In *The Spirit of the Alberta Indian Treaties,* edited by Richard T. Price. Edmonton: University of Alberta Press, 1999.

Funk, Jack. "Un Main Criminelle." In *Residential Schools: The Stolen Years,* edited by Linda Jaine. Saskatoon: University of Saskatchewan, University Extension Press, 1995.

Furniss, Elizabeth. *Victims of Benevolence: The Dark Legacy of the Williams Lake Residential School.* Vancouver: Arsenal Pulp Press, 1995.

George, Earl Maquinna. *Living on the Edge: Nuu-Chah-Nulth History of an Ahousaht Chief's Perspective.* Winlaw, BC: Sono Nis Press, 2003.

Gladstone, James. "Indian School Days." *Alberta Historical Review* 15, 1 (Winter 1967).

Gooderham, G.K. "Prospects." In *The Education of Indian Children in Canada: A Symposium,* edited by L.G.P. Waller. Toronto: The Ryerson Press, 1965.

Goodwill, Jean, and Norma Sluman, eds. *John Tootoosis.* Winnipeg: Pemmican Publications, 1984.

Graham, Angela. "Memorable Manitobans: Ahab Spence (1911–2001)." The Manitoba Historical Society, n.d. http://www.mhs.mb.ca/docs/people/spence_a.shtml (accessed 27 March 2011).

Graham, Elizabeth. *The Mush Hole: Life at Two Indian Residential Schools.* Waterloo: Heffle Publishing, 1997.

Grant, John Webster. *Moon of Wintertime: Missionaries and the Indians of Canada in Encounters since 1534.* Toronto: University of Toronto Press, 1985.

Gray, Richard, and Martine Gros-Louis Monier, eds. *Collection of Life Stories of the Survivors of the Quebec Indian Residential Schools.* Wendlake, QC: First Nations of Quebec and Labrador Health and Social Services Commission, 2010.

Gregoire, Edna. "Edna Gregoire." In *Behind Closed Doors: Stories from the Kamloops Indian Residential School,* edited by Agnes Jack. Secwepemc Cultural Education Society, Kamloops, British Columbia. Penticton: Theytus Books, 2006.

Gresko, Jacqueline. "Creating Little Dominions Within the Dominion: Early Catholic Indian Schools in Saskatchewan and British Columbia." In *Indian Education in Canada.* Vol. 1, *The Legacy,* edited by Jean Barman, Yvonne Hébert, and Don McCaskill. Vancouver: University of British Columbia Press, 1986.

_____. "Everyday Life at Qu'Appelle Industrial School," In *Western Oblate Studies 2,* edited by Raymond Huel. Lewiston: The Edwin Mellon Press, 1992.

_____. "Gender and Mission: the Founding Generations of the Sisters of Saint Ann and the Oblates of Mary Immaculate in British Columbia, 1858–1914." PhD dissertation, University of British Columbia, 1999.

Greyeyes, Harold. "The Day I Graduated." In *"… And then they told us their stories": A Book of Indian Stories,* edited by Jack Funk and Gordon Lobe. Saskatoon: Saskatoon District Tribal Council, 1991.

Guss, Lois. "Residential School Survivor." In *Residential Schools: The Stolen Years,* edited by Linda Jaine. Saskatoon: University of Saskatchewan, University Extension Press, 1995.

Hall, D.J. "Clifford Sifton and Canadian Indian Administration, 1896–1905." *Prairie Forum* 2 (1977).

Hamilton, John David. *Arctic Revolution: Social Change in the Northwest Territories, 1935–1994.* Toronto: Dundurn Press, 1994.

Hare, Jan, and Jean Barman. "Good Intentions Gone Awry: From Protection to Confinement in Emma Crosby's Home for Aboriginal Girls." In *Good Intentions: EuroCanadians and Aboriginal Relations in Colonial Canada,* edited by D. Nock and C. Haig-Brown. Vancouver: University of British Columbia Press, 2006.

Harrison, Julia D. *Metis: People between Two Worlds.* Calgary: Glenbow-Alberta Institute, 1985.

Harry. "Harry." In *Collection of Life Stories of the Survivors of the Quebec Indian Residential Schools,* edited by Richard Gray and Martine Gros-Louis Monier. Wendlake, QC: First Nations of Quebec and Labrador Health and Social Services Commission, 2010.

Hawthorn, H.B., ed. *A Survey of the Contemporary Indians of Canada: A Report on Economic, Political, Educational Needs and Policies.* Vol. 2. Ottawa: Indian Affairs Branch, 1967.

Henderson, James [sákéh] Youngblood. "Treaties and Indian Education." In *First Nations Education in Canada: The Circle Unfolds,* edited by Marie Battiste and Jean Barman. Vancouver: University of British Columbia Press, 1995.

Higham, C.L. *Noble, Wretched, and Redeemable: Protestant Missionaries to the Indians in Canada and the United States, 1820–1900.* Calgary: University of Calgary Press, 2000.

Hildebrand, Denise. "Staff Perspectives on the Aboriginal Residential School Experience: A Study of Four Presbyterian Schools, 1888–1923." Master of Sociology thesis, University of Manitoba, 2003.

Huel, Raymond J.A. *Proclaiming the Gospel to the Indians and Métis.* Edmonton: University of Alberta Press and Western Canadian Publishers, 1996.

Ignace, Ron. "Ron Ignace." In *Behind Closed Doors: Stories from the Kamloops Indian Residential School,* edited by Agnes Jack. Secwepemc Cultural Education Society, Kamloops, British Columbia. Penticton: Theytus Books, 2006.

Ignace, Vivian. "Vivian Ignace." In *Behind Closed Doors: Stories from the Kamloops Indian Residential School,* edited by Agnes Jack. Secwepemc Cultural Education

Society, Kamloops, British Columbia. Penticton: Theytus Books, 2006.

Indian Residential Schools Survivor Society. "About Our Society." http://www.irsss.ca/about_us.html (accessed 23 January 2011).

Irniq, Peter. "Peter Irniq." In *We Were So Far Away: The Inuit Experience of Residential Schools*, edited by Legacy of Hope Foundation. Ottawa: Legacy of Hope, 2010.

_____. "Remembering Ralph Ritcey's Compassion and Love." 5 December 2003. http://www.nunatsiaqonline.ca/archives/31219/opinionEditorial/letters.html (accessed 27 January 2011).

Jack, Agnes, ed. *Behind Closed Doors: Stories from the Kamloops Indian Residential School.* Secwepemc Cultural Education Society, Kamloops, British Columbia. Penticton: Theytus Books, 2006.

Jaenen, Cornelius J. "Education for Francization: The Case of New France in the Seventeenth Century." In *Indian Education in Canada.* Vol. 1, *The Legacy*, edited by Jean Barman, Yvonne Hébert, and Don McCaskill. Vancouver: University of British Columbia Press, 1986.

_____. *Friend and Foe: Aspects of French-Amerindian Cultural Contact in the Sixteenth and Seventeenth Centuries.* Toronto: McClelland and Stewart, Limited, 1973.

James, Mabel. "Then and Now." In *Residential Schools: The Stolen Years*, edited by Linda Jaine. Saskatoon: University of Saskatchewan, University Extension Press, 1995.

Jamplosky, L. "Advancement in Indian Education." In *The Education of Indian Children in Canada: A Symposium*, edited by L.G.P. Waller. Toronto: The Ryerson Press, 1965.

Janvier, Alphonse. "Alphonse Janvier." In *Métis Memories of Residential Schools: A Testament to the Strength of the Métis*, edited by Métis Nation of Alberta. Edmonton: Métis Nation of Alberta, 2004.

Joe, Rita, with the assistance of Lynn Henry. *Song of Rita Joe: Autobiography of a Mi´kmaq Poet.* Charlottetown: Ragweed Press, 1996.

Johnston, Basil H. *Indian School Days.* Toronto: Key Porter Books, 1988.

Johnston, Patrick. *Native Children and the Child Welfare System.* Toronto: Canadian Council on Social Development in association with J. Lorimer, 1983.

Johnston, Solomon. "We Didn't Learn Anything." In *"… And then they told us their stories": A Book of Indian Stories*, edited by Jack Funk and Gordon Lobe. Saskatoon: Saskatoon District Tribal Council, 1991.

Jules, Eddy. "Eddy Jules." In *Behind Closed Doors: Stories from the Kamloops Indian Residential School*, edited by Agnes Jack. Secwepemc Cultural Education Society, Kamloops, British Columbia. Penticton: Theytus Books, 2006.

Kelm, Mary-Ellen. "A Scandalous Procession: Residential Schooling and the Reformation of Aboriginal Bodies, 1900–1950." In *Children, Teachers, & Schools: In the History of British Columbia*, edited by Jean Barman, Neil Sutherland, and J.D. Wilson. Second edition, Calgary: Detselig Enterprises, 2003.

Kennedy, Daniel (Ochankugahe). *Recollections of an Assiniboine Chief.* Edited by James R. Stevens. Toronto: McClelland and Stewart, 1972.

King, A. Richard. *The School at Mopass: A Problem of Identity.* New York: Holt, Rinehart, and Winston, 1967.

King, David, "The History of the Federal Residential Schools for the Inuit Located in Chesterfield Inlet, Yellowknife, Inuvik and Churchill, 1955–1970." Master's thesis, Trent University, 1998.

_____. *A Brief Report of the Federal Government of Canada's Residential School System for Inuit.* Ottawa: Aboriginal Healing Foundation, 2006.

Knockwood, Isabelle. *Out of the Depths: The Experiences of Mi'kmaw Children at the Indian Residential School at Shubenacadie.* Roseway, NS: Fernwood, 2001.

Larocque, Archie. "Archie Larocque." In *Métis Memories of Residential Schools: A Testament to the Strength of the Métis*, edited by Métis Nation of Alberta. Edmonton: Métis Nation of Alberta, 2004.

LaViolette, Forrest. *The Struggle for Survival: Indian Cultures and the Protestant Ethic in British Columbia.* Toronto: University of Toronto Press, 1961.

Law Commission of Canada. *Restoring Dignity: Responding to Child Abuse in Canadian Institutions.* Ottawa: Minister of Public Works and Government Services, 2000.

Ledoux, Arthur. "Our Big Black Horse." In *"… And then they told us their stories": A Book of Indian Stories*, edited by Jack Funk and Gordon Lobe. Saskatoon: Saskatoon District Tribal Council, 1991.

Legacy of Hope Foundation, ed. *We Were So Far Away: The Inuit Experience of Residential Schools.* Ottawa: Legacy of Hope, 2010.

Logan, Tricia E. "'We were outsiders': The Métis and Residential Schools." Master of Arts thesis, University of Manitoba, 2007.

_____. "Lost Generations: The Silent Métis of the Residential School System Revised Interim Report." In *Métis History and Experience and Residential Schools in Canada*, edited by Larry N. Chartrand, Tricia E. Logan, and Judy D. Daniels. Ottawa: Aboriginal Healing Foundation, 2006.

Lux, Maureen K. *Medicine that Walks: Disease, Medicine and Canadian Plains Native People, 1880–1940.* Toronto: University of Toronto, 2001.

MacGregor, Roy. *Chief: The Fearless Vision of Billy Diamond.* Toronto: Viking, 1989.

MacLean, Hope. "Ojibwa Participation in Methodist Residential Schools in Upper Canada, 1828–1860." *The Canadian Journal of Native Studies* 25, 1 (2005).

Mandryk, Murray. "Uneasy Neighbours: White-Aboriginal Relations and Agricultural Decline." In *Writing Off the Rural West: Globalization, Governments and the Transformation of Rural Communities*, edited by Roger

Epp and Dave Whitson. Edmonton: University of Albert Press with the Parkland Institute, 2001.

Manuel, George, and Michael Posluns. *The Fourth World: An Indian Reality.* Toronto: Collier Macmillan Canada, 1974.

Manuel, Vera. "Abyss." In *Residential Schools: The Stolen Years,* edited by Linda Jaine. Saskatoon: University of Saskatchewan, University Extension Press, 1995.

Marchand, Janie. "Janie Marchand." In *Behind Closed Doors: Stories from the Kamloops Indian Residential School,* edited by Agnes Jack. Secwepemc Cultural Education Society, Kamloops, British Columbia. Penticton: Theytus Books, 2006.

Marguerite. "Marguerite." In *Collection of Life Stories of the Survivors of the Quebec Indian Residential Schools,* edited by Richard Gray and Martine Gros-Louis Monier. Wendlake, QC: First Nations of Quebec and Labrador Health and Social Services Commission, 2010.

McCarthy, Martha. *From the Great River to the Ends of the Earth: Oblate Missions to the Dene, 1847–1921.* Edmonton: University of Alberta Press, Western Canadian Publishers, 1995.

McGovern, Margaret. "Perspective on the Oblates: The Experience of the Sisters of Providence." *Western Oblate Studies* 3 (1994).

McMillan, Alan D., and Eldon Yellowhorn. *First Peoples in Canada.* Vancouver and Toronto: Douglas & McIntyre, 2004.

McPherson, Margaret E. "Head, Heart, and Purse: The Presbyterian Women's Missionary Society in Canada, 1876–1925." In *Prairie Spirit: Perspectives on the Heritage of the United Church of Canada in the West,* edited by Dennis L. Butcher, Catherine MacDonald, Margaret E. McPherson, Raymond R. Smith, and A. McKibbin Watts. Winnipeg: University of Manitoba Press, 1995.

Meltenberger, Theresa. "Theresa Meltenberger." In *Métis Memories of Residential Schools: A Testament to the Strength of the Métis,* edited by Métis Nation of Alberta. Edmonton: Métis Nation of Alberta, 2004.

Mercredi, Martha. "Martha Mercredi." In *Métis Memories of Residential Schools: A Testament to the Strength of the Métis,* edited by Métis Nation of Alberta. Edmonton: Métis Nation of Alberta, 2004.

Métis Nation of Alberta, ed. *Métis Memories of Residential Schools: A Testament to the Strength of the Métis.* Edmonton: Métis Nation of Alberta, 2004.

Miller, J.R. *Compact, Contract, Covenant: Aboriginal Treaty Making in Canada.* Toronto: University of Toronto Press, 2009.

———. *Shingwauk's Vision: A History of Native Residential Schools.* Toronto: University of Toronto Press, 1996.

Milloy, John S. "The Early Indian Acts: Developmental Strategy and Constitutional Change." In *As Long as the Sun Shines and Water Flows,* edited by Ian L. Getty and Antoine S. Lussier. Vancouver: University of British Columbia Press, 1983.

———. *A National Crime: The Canadian Government and the Residential School System, 1879 to 1986.* Winnipeg: University of Manitoba Press, 1999.

Mitchell, Allan. "Allan Mitchell." In *Behind Closed Doors: Stories from the Kamloops Indian Residential School,* edited by Agnes Jack. Secwepemc Cultural Education Society, Kamloops, British Columbia. Penticton: Theytus Books, 2006.

Moore, A. "The Teaching Staff in Indian Schools." In *The Education of Indian Children in Canada: A Symposium,* edited by L.G.P. Waller. Toronto: The Ryerson Press, 1965.

Moore, Robert G., John Leslie, and Ron Maguire. *The Historical Development of the Indian Act.* Ottawa: Treaties and Historical Research Centre, P.R.E. Group, Indian and Northern Affairs, 1978.

Moorhouse, Geoffrey. *The Missionaries.* Philadelphia and New York: J.B. Lippincott Company, 1973.

Moran, Bridget. *Stoney Creek Woman: The Story of Mary John.* Vancouver: Arsenal Pulp Press, 1997.

Morantz, Toby. *The White Man's Gonna Getcha: The Colonial Challenge to the Crees in Quebec.* Montreal and Kingston: McGill-Queen's University Press, 2002.

Morley, Alan. *Roar of the Breakers: A Biography of Peter Kelly.* Toronto: The Ryerson Press, 1967.

Morris, Alexander. *The Treaties of Canada with the Indians of Manitoba and the North-West Territories, Including the Negotiations on Which They Were Based.* 1880. Reprint, Saskatoon: Fifth House, 1991.

Mountain Horse. *Mike, My People, The Bloods.* Calgary: Glenbow Museum, 1979.

National Residential Schools Survivors' Society. http://www.nrsss.ca (accessed 23 January 2011).

Niviaxie, Carolyn. "Carolyn Niviaxie." In *We Were So Far Away: The Inuit Experience of Residential Schools,* edited by Legacy of Hope Foundation. Ottawa: Legacy of Hope, 2010.

PeeAce, John. "We Almost Won." In *"… And then they told us their stories": A Book of Indian Stories,* edited by Jack Funk and Gordon Lobe. Saskatoon: Saskatoon District Tribal Council, 1991.

Peequaquat, George, "We Missed the Bus." In *"… And then they told us their stories": A Book of Indian Stories,* edited by Jack Funk and Gordon Lobe. Saskatoon: Saskatoon District Tribal Council, 1991.

Peikoff, Tannis, and Stephen Brickey. "Creating Precious Children and Glorified Mothers: A Theoretical Assessment of the Transformation of Childhood in Canada." In *Dimensions of Childhood: Essays on the History of Children and Youth in Canada,* edited by Russell Smandych, Gordon Dodds, and Alvin Esau. Winnipeg: Legal Research Institute of the University of Manitoba, 1991.

Persson, Diane. "The Changing Experience of Indian Residential Schooling: Blue Quills, 1931–1970." In *Indian Education in Canada.* Vol. 1, *The Legacy,* edited by Jean

Barman, Yvonne Hébert, and Don McCaskill. Vancouver: University of British Columbia Press, 1986.

Peterson, Katherine. *Sir Joseph Bernier Federal Day School, Turquetil Hall Investigation Report.* Yellowknife: Government of the Northwest Territories, 1994.

Pettipas, Katherine. *Severing the Ties that Bind: Government Repression of Indigenous Religious Ceremonies on the Prairies.* Winnipeg: University of Manitoba Press, 1994.

Pettit, Jennifer Lorretta. "'To Christianize and Civilize': Native Industrial Schools in Canada." PhD dissertation, University of Calgary, 1997.

Phillips, R.A.J. *Canada's North.* Toronto: Macmillan of Canada, 1967.

Quiring, David M. *CCF Colonialism in Northern Saskatchewan: Battling Parish Priests, Bootleggers, and Fur Sharks.* Vancouver: University of British Columbia Press, 2004.

Raibmon, Paige. "'A New Understanding of Things Indian': George Raley's Negotiation of the Residential School Experience." *BC Studies* 110 (Summer 1996).

Ray, Arthur, Jim Miller, and Frank Tough. *Bounty and Benevolence: A History of Saskatchewan Indian Treaties.* Montreal: McGill-Queen's University Press, 2000.

Redford, James W. "Attendance at Indian Residential Schools in British Columbia, 1890–1920." Master of History thesis, University of British Columbia, 1978.

Roberts, Donna. "Donna Roberts." In *Métis Memories of Residential Schools: A Testament to the Strength of the Métis,* edited by Métis Nation of Alberta. Edmonton: Métis Nation of Alberta, 2004.

Rompkey, William. *The Story of Labrador.* Montreal and Kingston: McGill-Queen's University Press, 2003.

Ruben, Abraham. "Abraham Ruben." In *We Were So Far Away: The Inuit Experience of Residential Schools,* edited by Legacy of Hope Foundation. Ottawa: Legacy of Hope, 2010.

Rutherdale, Myra. "Mothers of the Empire: Maternal Metaphors in the Northern Canadian Mission Field." In *Canadian Missionaries, Indigenous Peoples: Representing Religion at Home and Abroad,* edited by Alvyn Austin and Jamie S. Scott. Toronto: University of Toronto Press, 2005.

_____. *Women and the White Man's God: Gender and Race in the Canadian Mission Field.* Vancouver: University of British Columbia Press, 2002.

Sanderson, Geraldine. "Running Away." In "*… And then they told us their stories": A Book of Indian Stories,* edited by Jack Funk and Gordon Lobe. Saskatoon: Saskatoon District Tribal Council, 1991.

Sandy, Ralph. "Ralph Sandy." In *Behind Closed Doors: Stories from the Kamloops Indian Residential School,* edited by Agnes Jack. Secwepemc Cultural Education Society, Kamloops, British Columbia. Penticton: Theytus Books, 2006.

Schmalz, Peter S. *The Ojibwa of Southern Ontario.* Toronto: University of Toronto Press, 1991.

Schroeder, Geraldine. "Geraldine Schroeder." In *Behind Closed Doors: Stories from the Kamloops Indian Residential School,* edited by Agnes Jack. Secwepemc Cultural Education Society, Kamloops, British Columbia. Penticton: Theytus Books, 2006.

Scott, Duncan Campbell. "Indian Affairs 1867–1912." In *Canada and its Provinces.* Vol. 7, edited by A. Shortt and A. Doughty. Toronto: University of Edinburgh Press, 1913.

Sellars, Bev. "Survival Against All Odds." In *Residential Schools: The Stolen Years,* edited by Linda Jaine. Saskatoon: University of Saskatchewan, University Extension Press, 1995.

Shaw, Magee. "Magee Shaw." In *Métis Memories of Residential Schools: A Testament to the Strength of the Métis,* edited by Métis Nation of Alberta. Edmonton: Métis Nation of Alberta, 2004.

Shea, Goldie. *Institutional Child Abuse in Canada: Criminal Cases.* Ottawa: Law Commission of Canada, 1999.

Sheni7. "Sheni7" in "Ralph Sandy." In *Behind Closed Doors: Stories from the Kamloops Indian Residential School,* edited by Agnes Jack. Secwepemc Cultural Education Society, Kamloops, British Columbia. Penticton: Theytus Books, 2006.

Shingwauk, Augustine. *Little Pine's Journal: The Appeal of a Christian Chippeway Chief on Behalf of his People.* Toronto: Copp, Clark, 1872.

Smith, Donald. "F.O. Loft." In *Dictionary of Canadian Biography.* http://www.biographi.ca/009004-119.01-e.php?&id_nbr=8419&&PHPSESSID=vzofxpjx (accessed 21 August 2011).

Smith, Donald. "Fred Loft." In *Encyclopedia of North American Indians,* edited by Frederick E. Hoxie. Boston: Houghton Mifflin, 1996.

_____. *Sacred Feathers: The Reverend Peter Jones (Kahkewaquonaby) and the Mississauga Indians.* Toronto: University of Toronto Press, 1987.

Speare, Jean E., ed. *The Days of Augusta.* Vancouver: J.J. Douglas, 1973.

Stanley, George F.G. "Alberta's Half-Breed Reserve Saint-Paul-des-Métis, 1896–1909." In *The Other Natives: The Métis.* Vol. 2, edited by A.S. Lussier and D.B. Sealey. Winnipeg: Manitoba Métis Federation Press, 1978.

Stanley, George F.G. *Louis Riel.* Toronto: The Ryerson Press, 1963.

Stevenson, Winona. "The Red River Indian Mission School and John West's 'Little Charges' 1820–1833." *Native Studies Review* 4, nos. 1 and 2 (1988).

Sutherland, Neil. *Children in English-Canadian Society: Framing the Twentieth-Century Consensus.* Waterloo: Wilfrid Laurier University Press, 2000.

Taylor, John Leonard. "Canada's Northwest Indian Policy in the 1870s: Traditional Premises and Necessary Innovations." In *The Spirit of the Alberta Indian Treaties,* edited by Richard T. Price. Edmonton: University of Alberta Press, 1999.

Thomas, James. "James Thomas." In *Métis Memories of Residential Schools: A Testament to the Strength of the Métis*, edited by Métis Nation of Alberta. Edmonton: Métis Nation of Alberta, 2004.

Thommasen, Harvey, ed. *Grizzlies and White Guys: The Stories of Clayton Mack*. Vancouver: Harbour Publishing, 1993.

Thomson-Millward, Marilyn. "Researching the Devils: A Study of Brokerage at the Indian Residential School, Shubenacadie, Nova Scotia." PhD dissertation, Dalhousie University, 1997.

Thrasher, Anthony Apakark. *Thrasher: Skid Row Eskimo*. Toronto: Griffin House, 1976.

Titley, E. Brian. "Dunbow Indian Industrial School: An Oblate Experiment in Education." In *Western Oblate Studies 2*, edited by Raymond Huel. Lewiston: The Edwin Mellon Press, 1992.

_____. "Hayter Reed and Indian Administration in the West." In *Swords and Ploughshares: War and Agriculture in Western Canada*, edited by R.C. MacLeod. Edmonton: University of Alberta Press, 1993.

_____. "Indian Industrial Schools in Western Canada." In *Schools in the West: Essays in Canadian Educational History*, edited by Nancy M. Sheehan, J. Donald Wilson, and David C. Jones. Calgary: Detselig, 1986.

_____. *A Narrow Vision: Duncan Campbell Scott and the Administration of Indian Affairs in Canada*. Vancouver: University of British Columbia Press, 1986.

_____. "Red Deer Industrial School: A Case Study in the History of Native Education." In *Exploring Our Educational Past: Schooling in the North-West Territories and Alberta*, edited by Nick Kach and Kas Mazurek. Calgary: Detselig Enterprises, 1992.

Tizya, Clara. "Comment." *In The Education of Indian Children in Canada: A Symposium*, edited by L.G.P. Waller. Toronto: The Ryerson Press, 1965.

Tobias, John L. "Canada's Subjugation of the Plains Cree, 1879–1885." In *Sweet Promises: A Reader on Indian-White Relations in Canada*, edited by J.R. Miller. Toronto: University of Toronto Press, 1991.

Tungilik, Marius. "Marius Tungilik." In *We Were So Far Away: The Inuit Experience of Residential Schools*, edited by Legacy of Hope Foundation. Ottawa: Legacy of Hope, 2010.

Usher, Jean. *William Duncan of Metlakatla: A Victorian Missionary in British Columbia*. Publications in History, No. 9. Ottawa: National Museums of Canada, 1974.

Van Camp, Rose. "Paul Piché." *Arctic* 42, 2 (1989).

Wachowich, Nancy, in collaboration with Apphia Agalakti Awa, Rhoda Kaukjak Katsak, and Sandra Pikujak Katsak. *Saqiyuq: Stories from the Lives of Three Inuit Women*. Montreal and Kingston: McGill-Queen's University Press, 1999.

Waldram, James, D. Ann Herring, and T. Kue Young. *Aboriginal Health in Canada: Historical, Cultural, and Epidemiological Perspectives*. Second edition, Toronto: University of Toronto Press, 2006.

Weetaltuk, Salamiva. "Salamiva Weetaltuk." In *We Were So Far Away: The Inuit Experience of Residential Schools*, edited by Legacy of Hope Foundation. Ottawa: Legacy of Hope, 2010.

Wherrett, George Jasper. *The Miracle of the Empty Beds: A History of Tuberculosis in Canada*. Toronto: University of Toronto Press, 1977.

Whitehead, Margaret. "Introduction." *They Call Me Father: Memoirs of Father Nicolas Coccola*. Edited by Margaret Whitehead. Vancouver: University of British Columbia Press, 1988.

Willis, Jane. *Geniesh: An Indian Girlhood*. Toronto: New Press, 1973.

Sources of quotations in captions

Page 6: House of Commons, Debates, 46 Victoria, 9 May 1883, 14: 1107-08, quoted in Blair Stonechild, *The New Buffalo: The Struggle for Aboriginal Post-Secondary Education in Canada*. Winnipeg: University of Manitoba Press, 2006, 9.

Page 9: George M. Wrong, editor, *The Long Journey to the Country of the Huron by Father Gabriel Sagard*, Toronto: 1939, 130–131, quoted in Cornelius Jaenen, *Friend and Foe Aspects of French-Amerindian Cultural Contact in the Sixteenth and Seventeenth Centuries*. Toronto: McClelland and Stewart, Limited, 1973, 94.

Page 12: File 470-2-3, volume 7, Evidence of D.C. Scott to the Special Committee of the House of Commons Investigating the *Indian Act* amendments of 1920, 63 (N-3), quoted in Robert G. Moore, John Leslie, and Ron Maguire, *The Historical Development of the Indian Act*, Ottawa: Treaties and Historical Research Centre, P.R.E. Group, Indian and Northern Affairs, 1978, 114.

Page 14: John Maclean, *The Indians: Their Manners and Customs*, Toronto Methodist Mission Rooms, 1889, 264, quoted in C.L. Higham, *Noble, Wretched, and Redeemable: Protestant Missionaries to the Indians in Canada and the United States, 1820-1900*. Calgary: University of Calgary Press, 2000, 59.

Page 22: Susan E. Gray, *I Will Fear No Evil: Ojibwa-missionary Encounters Along the Berens River, 1875-1940*. Calgary: University of Calgary Press, 2006, 8.

Page 23: Library and Archives Canada, RG 10, Volume 8449, File 511/23-5-014, MR C 13800, Inspection Report, Birtle School, by A.G. Hamilton, 4 December 1936, quoted in John Milloy, *A National Crime: The Canadian Government and the Residential School System, 1879 to 1986*. Winnipeg: University of Manitoba Press, 1999, 123.

Page 30: P.H. Bryce, *Report on the Indian Schools of Manitoba and the North-West Territories*. Ottawa: Government Printing Bureau, 1907, 20-21.

Page 31: Library and Archives Canada, RG 10, Volume 3674, File 11422, MR C 10118 Rev. J. Hugonnard to E. Dewdney, 5 May 1891, quoted in John Milloy, *A National Crime: The Canadian Government and the Residential School System, 1879 to 1986*. Winnipeg: University of Manitoba Press, 1999, 116.

Page 37: Library and Archives Canada, RG 10, Volume 6267, File 580-1, (103), MR C 8656, J. Waddy to W. Graham, 1 September 1924, quoted in John Milloy, *A National Crime: The Canadian Government and the Residential School System, 1879 to 1986*. Winnipeg: University of Manitoba Press, 1999, 147.

Page 40: Simon Baker, *Khot-La-Cha: The Autobiography of Chief Simon Baker*, compiled and edited by Verna J. Kirkness, Vancouver: Douglas and McIntyre, 1994, 33–34.

Page 46: Andsell Macrae, Inspector Protestant Indian Schools, Sessional Papers, 1889, Paper 16, 146–147, quoted in Walter Julian Wasylow, "History of Battleford Industrial School for Indians," Masters of Education thesis, University of Saskatchewan, 1972, 90–91.

Page 66: Jack Bumsted, *Louis Riel v. Canada*, Winnipeg: Great Plains, 2001, 237.

Page 77: Jane Willis, *Geniesh: An Indian Girlhood*, Toronto: New Press, 1973, 136; 161.